"DEAD AIR"

How the radio business can once again thrive by embracing all of the existing and coming social media technologies

DAVID LEAR

iUniverse, Inc.
New York   Bloomington

"DEAD AIR"
How the radio business can once again thrive by embracing all of the existing and coming social media technologies

iUniverse books may be ordered through booksellers or by contacting:

iUniverse
1663 Liberty Drive
Bloomington, IN 47403
www.iuniverse.com
1-800-Authors (1-800-288-4677)

Because of the dynamic nature of the Internet, any Web addresses or links contained in this book may have changed since publication and may no longer be valid.

ISBN: 978-1-4502-1694-4 (sc)
ISBN: 978-1-4502-1695-1 (ebk)

Printed in the United States of America

iUniverse rev. date: 3/8/2010

FOREWORD

My fifteen-year career in the radio business has been relatively brief (so far) by some standards. I've met some 30, 40 and even 50-year veterans of this "entertainment business." Yet my perspective is based on the lucky confluence of when I started on the cusp of 1994-95 to the present 2009-10 since my career began just before the infamous "Telecommunications Act" of 1996. This changed the whole ball game in which one owner/operator was allowed to own many media properties in the same market. Previous to my experience there was only allowed a "duopoly" where one owner was limited to one radio station and maybe one TV station in the same market, or one AM radio signal and one FM signal per market.

That began to change around the time I entered the business and the 1996 act marked both the Federal government getting involved in the affairs of free enterprise and capitalism. We all know how that usually works out!

THE POST OFFICE: BROKE!

MEDICARE AND MEDICAID: BROKE!
SOCIAL SECURITY: BROKE!
RADIO CONSOLODATORS: I'LL LET YOU TAKE
A GUESS!

I've met a great many tremendously talented, loyal and dedicated individuals in these past 15 years yet I've also encountered some of the lowest life scum in this, or any other galaxy in the universe. And I speak from experience since I've visited these other galaxies!

I've heard the expression many times, under many circumstances, and in many states across this nation:

"We believe that our employees are our greatest asset." This is basically a humorous autobiographical account of my journey through those 15 tumultuous and rapidly changing years in the business and the story of how some of those same totally shallow, completely phony, big bags of hot air proceeded to squander their "assets" like a drunken cowboy at a Las Vegas cat house!

This is not meant to be a 'tell all' memoir or some kind of "Bobby Dearest" blast at any one person or group. In fact as the 15 chapters' progress you'll be introduced to many positive and truly exciting ways that the industry can both survive and again thrive,

The premise is actually fairly simple. In their dreams to build what they called "shareholder value" these 'captains of industry' simply took their eye off the ball. They said repeatedly that their aim was to serve their three main groups of customers:

1. Their listeners.
2. Their advertisers.

3. Their employees.

Instead they knelt at the altar of their stockholders and investors and made every move, every decision, and every tweak to satisfy their bottom line, to "save money" and basically snatched the heart and soul out of what made radio so great; its unique ability to be both live and local, a well-known friend, a close part of your everyday life. In this process they did a great disservice to the three aforementioned groups of "customers", They watered down the content and made it so bland and homogenous, while at the same time ignoring some key sociological and technological trends that were greatly accelerating all around them. They now stand to lose an entire generation of listeners. This is also the largest generation the world has ever seen. They're even larger than even the "baby boomers." These are "The Millenials" or "Generation Y." 80 million strong they will soon be entering into what most advertising agencies value as gold. They'll be entering a certain 'sweet spot' where they tend to be the heaviest consumers who purchase the most of everything that advertisers are selling. They'll be entering that "golden demographic" of "adults 25-54 years of age." They don't like radio in its current form, have much shorter attention spans, as do all age groups today due to rapid advances in technology and informational delivery systems, and are becoming their own program directors as they load their iPods with the music they prefer to listen to, totally customized and totally commercial free. This isn't just a challenge to the radio business. How many folks of all ages "TiVo" their television shows to watch, also commercial free, when their individual hectic, modern schedules permit?

Each and every name, place, station, city, group cluster, and individual name has been changed to protect the innocent as well as the untold numbers of the guilty. And any resemblance to any person, place or situation, living or dead, is purely coincidental. Consider this a work of fiction. And then use your own common sense. Listen to your gut.

So now strap yourself in and take a roller coaster ride of laughs as we enter the world of volume one of 'DEAD AIR."

Respectfully,
David Lear

Contents

CHAPTER ONE

One sunny March morning general sales manager Matthew Garcia was bounced down three flights of stairs and out into the parking lot on his ass from "Crux Communications" in Tampa, Florida. The "three flight bounce" was just a metaphor, an inside joke of an expression we were all using since this had become almost a weekly phenomena in Tampa both from Crux as well as their consolidated competitors, all throughout 2008 and 2009 as the recession deepened.

Matt was one of the most intelligent, creative, successful, educated and knowledgeable managers I had ever had the pleasure of working for. And with a black belt in Kung-Fu as well as history of being a successful boxer, the "stair bounce" would have taken me as well as several other 200 pound men to even come close to achieve.

It was, of course, to "save money" for the company since Matthew had negotiated a salary far superior to some other managers at the company and was thus an 'easy target' as he put it. And he was worth it. He had more then doubled the average commercial rate for the radio station we both worked for since we both began our careers there in 2004. I had 'retired' the month before to write this book.

During the same period of time somewhere in Nebraska, again to save money, another one of the huge consolidators, "Carrier Wave Communications" was enthusiastically encouraging the listeners to their country station to "come on down here, y'all!!" to the fairgrounds where a huge country music fest was about to take place. Trouble was that, again to 'save money' the announcements had been pre-recorded two weeks prior and didn't take into account the reality of the current weather situation. A huge hurricane was about to touch down right in the middle of the venue. Despite frantic warnings from the National Weather service, the fans ignored the 'breaking news', totally bought into the content of the two week old announcements, supposedly "live" and over 300 cars ended up under water or heavily damaged with mud as the banks of a neighboring river overflowed, the performers had long abandoned the stage and were "hunkered down" in their tour buses. It took 36 towing companies and the threat of a class action lawsuit for "Carrier Wave" to finally let go of their 'act of God' cowardice excuses and make good on all of the damages, well into the hundreds of thousands of dollars. Not to mention the skull cracked open of one fan, who dove from his vehicle into the torrent to retrieve his false buck teeth, smashing his head open on a boulder hidden by the rushing waters.

Within the same month a business manager, a lady who had been at "Nimbus" Communications for 13 years, drove into her garage, knowing that she HAD to quit her position since the cameras and the 'big brother' monitoring of every employee's every keystroke, every computer action and every phone call---along with constant harassing threats from upper management each day---had broken her down into a semi catatonic state. She knew she had to quit but also knew that she'd lose her house if she did. So she simply left her car running and hit the garage door remote, quickly succumbing to carbon monoxide death. What happened with this once thriving business?

CHAPTER TWO

HOW IT ALL EVOLVED AND WHEN I "JUMPED IN" TO THE BUSINESS RIGHT AT THE 'FOCAL POINT."

I began my first radio position as an "A.E." or "account executive" in 1995, slightly more precisely during the weeks leading up to 1995 during the last two weeks of 1994 when they required us to be 'role-playing' both on Christmas eve as well on New year's eve of 1994. But I'm getting a bit ahead of myself.

To fully grasp the development of the radio industry let's start with a very brief, "Reader's Digest" version of how the business developed.

1. Guglielo Marconi transmitted Morse code through the air in 1901. Used primarily as a ship to shore communication. It replaced the previous messaging with flags on larger ships by the US

Navy, greatly enhancing communications. And on one tragic day in April 1912 a signal was picked up, an "S-O-S" from the doomed super liner, the Titanic. The young wireless receiver, David Sarnoff, later founded the Radio Corporation of America (RCA), and dreamed of future that would be led by a "radio music box" that would bring music into homes through tubes and speakers. By 1922 his invention was complete and the music boxes were sold for around $70 and stared to be fixtures in American homes.

2. COMMERCIAL Radio. The commercial radio stations began to pop up on the AM dial. The first one, KDKA Pittsburg was licensed in 1919 and began operations out of a tent. There were only two commercial radio stations in 1921. Less than a year later more than 200 stations were reaching an audience of over 3 million homes. One of these was to be my first radio position; I'll call it "WFZ" out of Schenectady, New York. Despite all of the 'buzz" the original operators had difficulty finding an economic model or ways to earn income. The first radio commercial was a ten-minute announcement for a real estate company in New York in 1922. Still there was not a flood of advertisers getting on board. In 1923 several radio stations were connected by phone lines and tried identical broadcasts at the same time and thus networking was born. Sarnoff jumped on this band wagon and created the NBC radio network in 1926, serving 24 stations. Such networks allowed broadcasters to create programs

all over the country featuring some of America's biggest stars. Thus the "Golden Age" of radio came about and in the years leading up to World War Two a wide universe of programs, featuring former vaudeville stars, Jack Benny, Bob Hope, Burns and Allen arrived on the scene. By the war radio was America's premier communications medium. Advertising dollars started to pour in during this period lading up to the conflict and beyond.

3. TV CHALLENGES. In 1948 TV began to be licensed and the emerging industry grew quickly and much management, staff, and talent rushed into the new medium, forcing radio to change to meet consumer and advertiser demands in an increasingly competitive environment. In response to television radio became more intimate and personal and the format concept was born!!!

4. FM RADIO COMES ON THE SCENE. In the late 1960's some creative folks began to see the upside of the largely inactive FM band. The AM signal could generally travel further due to the "Carrier Wave effect" of AM or amplitude modulation where the signal bounced off the ionosphere of the earth, back onto the ground, and again into the ionosphere, to the ground and hence could travel for hundreds of miles with a powerful enough signal. FM or 'frequency modulation' was generally limited to the line of sight but produced a fuller, richer, sound reproduction more conducive to music broadcast. This is why most "news/talk" formats

are AM while most music formats are FM. Radio eventually entered the car market technology, exponentially increasing total listening. Radio began to experience tremendous financial growth. Then, the most pivotal moment in the entire radio industry quietly, yet significantly, in the long run, arrived!!!

5. THE 1996 TELECOMMUNICATIONS ACT. Government intrusion into the free market system? Now why does that seem so familiar these days?!! As a result of this act broadcasters were allowed to own significantly more signals per market than they had been able to previously. One positive aspect was to allow radio companies to offer advertisers unprecedented access to high focused consumer lifestyle groups. The destructive negatives are the main focus of this little ditty.

Along with all of the technological developments, Radio programming in general has traveled through three significant programming eras since 1920.

A. The Big Band Period of approximately 1920-1948. This era was similar to what TV is today. These were blocks of 15, 30, or 60-minute programs. Radio sold sponsorships to advertisers for these block segments. Stations also allowed the local announcer to select the music, management-free and geared to what the advertiser felt could generate the most entertainment and to what the audience loved listening to the most.

B. THE FORMAT CONCEPT, Circa 1949-early 1960's. Looking for a significant way to boldly differentiate itself from TV, radio conceived of a specialization which changed the game from offering all types of programming for all types of people on one station, to various radio formats or styles of programming all day long or for at least very long periods of time. The very first I barely remember was "Top 40" or as they call it today, Contemporary Hit radio or CHR. At the same time the thrust of radio sales changed from selling sponsorships to whole programs to selling individual commercials or "spot sales." The formats ran the gamut: "Middle of the road" (MOR), Country, Rhythm and Blues, Gospel, Beautiful Music" (easy listening), News/talk, Classical, etc. It was around this time that the position of "PD" or program director was emerging. Many program "tactics" came of age during this period that are still used today that include commercial clusters and long music "sweeps." You recognize them. "45 minutes of uninterrupted music' followed by "15 minutes of uninterrupted commercials."

C. RADIO MEASURES AUDIENCE QUANTITY, circa early 1960's to today. How many of us remember the agonizing, fake enthusiastic, overly loud and "in your face" "DJ'" yelling over the beginning and endings of songs? What started out as merely total number of all listeners over 12 or over 18 gradually evolved into specific demographic 'cells'(or ranges), gender, and lifestyle. By the use of "Arbitron" diaries, similar to household measurement by TV in its Neilson ratings, and then the use of actual 20-minute household phone surveys to measure lifestyle; income, planning to buy, currently using, driving, etc. radio stations had a more clear picture of who their listeners actually were. But sending out, say, 1,800 diaries to measure the listening habits of a "metro" (or immediate geographical listening area of, say 2.3 million people, was almost statistically meaningless since these statistics had a plus or minus accuracy of 5-7% rendering them nearly useless mathematically. I can remember once in the Tampa Bay "metro" of Tampa, Saint Petersburg, and Clearwater, Florida there were 14 different stations and formats that fell within ONE TENTH of one rating point of one another! This left the poor, unsophisticated, usually barely trained sales staff to ALL claim that their particular station was "number one!" And indeed they were. In fact by ever so slightly manipulating the figures almost every one of them could show that they were indeed "number one" somewhere!

In fact, national sales consultant, Dr. Phillip LeNoble, used to go into the field, sarcastically illustrating this when he told potential advertisers: "Did you know that in this market we have 31 "number one" radio stations?!!" It didn't take a statistician to realize that this type of "measurement" was totally bogus but guess what most advertisers and advertising agencies utilized as "the Bible" for making their advertising decisions? You guessed it! "Arbitron diaries!!"

Most recently introduced has been the "People Meter." In this case some poor sap agrees to have a device strapped to their belt that picks up encoded radio signals wherever they may go.

Now think about THIS work of "genius" for a second. Say a 16-year old, who listeners and prefers nothing but 'rap' music spends a few hours in a hospital, doctor's or dentist's office, and thus has 'beautiful, easy, relaxing' oldies music being picked up by his "People meter." He will thus be counted and weighed as being an easy listening (or even big band era!) listener when in reality he's nothing of the sort! The ultimate answer and the only real means of growth and new account development since I went out "on the road" in the radio business in 1995 was the golden goose value of new, direct account development. These folks didn't give, as General George Patton allegedly said. "a hoot in hell" about ratings points or who, using some ridiculous statistical method, was "number one." They wanted only to grow their business, to gain market share, to have a successful media campaign and a measurable return on their investment. And who wouldn't? In ANY situation involving investments or ANYTHING involving one's hard-earned money?!! This is the environment I entered in 1995 in radio, right before the 1996 TELECOMMUNICATIONS ACT and the advent of market consolidation.

Let's start out in late 1994 when my father, a loyal news/talk listener to news/talk powerhouse, "WFZ" heard a radio ad announcing interviews for radio sales people. He told me about it since he knew I was a creative writer, song composer with over 300 original tunes under my belt, and a great deal of successful sales experience as a wholesale food distributor salesman both in Schenectady, New York, and then later in Los Angles California where I had arrived in 1984 on a one-way ticket, with no car, no job prospects, and just $1,500 to my name and an American Express credit card in my wallet. Working 7-day weeks I had, four years later, purchased, with my brother and his wife as equal partners, 50/50 with me, a 4-plex on the beach that was appraised at $936,000. It's a matter of public record. 1617 Seal Way, Seal Beach, California, 90740. I was on the deed as owner from 1988 to 1991. Look it up.

Hit in a 5-car pile up on one of the busiest freeways in L.A. the "Long Beach Freeway" (710) at 55mph, I was lucky to be alive, but while on disability my company folded and after racking up over 250,000 miles on the freeways of L.A. I was in need of a breather and returned, after selling my share in the 4-plex to my brother and his wife, to upstate New York.

I responded to the ad for a sales position on WFZ but was told that the positions had all been filled. However, not 90-days later my father told me that they were once again running the same sales position announcements. "A few people must not have worked out": I thought. What an understatement THAT turned out to be!!!

CHAPTER THREE

THE EARLY YEARS IN THE "GREAT NORTHEAST."

Now let's all agree on the obvious. No business model is perfect. No business is run perfectly either. Please excuse the tautology here when I tell you that I didn't want this book to sound like some kind of "tell all" or "Bobby Dearest" where I'm constantly perceived as "going negative." As Bob Dylan answered an interviewer who asked if he was an angry man since he seemed angry in most of his songs he replied: "Actually I'm a delightful sort of person." We're all human, we all make mistakes. That's our very nature. But we're also supposed to learn something from those mistakes.

My overall experience in 15 years in the radio business has revealed a number of patterns of behavior; the classic definition of insanity as doing the same thing over and over and expecting a different result.

Thus let me illuminate some of my experiences as I entered the radio industry in December of 1994, starting with the interview process. My sales experience had been in the wholesale food business as a distributor salesman who sold a catalogue of over 5,000 items to any entity that would use them: Restaurants, hotels, military bases, cafeterias, caterers, banquet halls, hospitals, nursing homes, schools and on and on. So my first "hard-hitting" questions from the general manager/V.P. of WFZ as well as the station general manager involved the sale of tangibles, such as food items as opposed to intangible items such as airtime or commercial inventory. They asked me the same question several times and in several different ways, which I thought to be a little ridiculous after the third time. But as they frantically scribbled down my answer it was always the same.

Yes I had sold tangible assets but before I could do that I had to make several intangible sales first. I had to sell myself and my own credibility, competence, professionalism and reliability. Then I had to sell the same features of my company, especially their overall service to their customers as well as the consistency and the quality of the products, delivery, and inventory control and trouble-shooting to solve the operator's problems. The actual price, although one main consideration was rarely at the top of the list. Thus the 'selling" was truly at the essence of what I did, the rest became basically order-taking and suggesting and demonstrating or sampling new products as they came on the market. These people were running a business and they were basically looking for a reliable business "partner."

I was hired after several interviews with two other individuals out of a pool of applicants that numbered in the hundreds, at least. The starting salary was just $1,700 per month and it was reduced by $100 in each succeeding month to be replaced and increased as we brought in new business and opened new advertising accounts. Sure they were trying to 'do it on the cheap' but I had unlimited faith, from my success in the food industry, that new business development had always been my strongest suit and that I had always led the field in new business creation, no matter where I worked in the industry. It's sort of a continuous, self- feeding loop. If you really love and have a passion for what you do you'll excel at it, see results, and thus become self-motivated to succeed at it over and over again. What's that old expression? Nothing succeeds like success?

THE TRAINING

The three of us sat every day for a month in a darkened room, while a series of training tapes were played in sequential order. But even before that we had to write a brief "sales presentation" on why the company should hire us, our first 'sale.' Then something happened that awakened my first vague feeling that the focus was somewhere OTHER than on the lives of the salespeople.

It seems as if their "training schedule" was tight for some reason, and just HAD to be completed by the first of the year, January 1st, 1995. So as unbelievable at this may sound, they had us in the office 'role playing' ("O.k. I'm the head of a huge dental practice. Now show me how you'd approach me to make an appointment, give

me a valid business reason for me to meet with you!")
Etc. The incredible part of this schedule was that we had
to be there 'role playing' on both Christmas Eve as well
as on New Year's eve of 1994!!

The faces of several of my friends were contorted like
smashed Halloween masks as they kept asking me: "You
were actually in there 'ROLE PLAYING' on BOTH
Christmas Eve AND New Year's Eve? Why?!!! Didn't they
think you had a life?!!"

It was one of those instances in which if it wasn't so
sad it'd be funny. And I can actually laugh at it now!
Guys who were 3 or 4 months into their new radio
"careers", such as one gentleman named Tom Cook, in
particular, already seemed quite disillusioned over the
whole process, telling us that: "What your watching
in there is theory...it's not the real world out there!"
Tom was subsequently taken into the general manager's
office where he underwent some intensive "role playing"
training and 'washed out' of the business about a month
later. In fact the receptionist told us that the three
station group in Schenectady was burning through one
salesperson each month. And out of a sales staff of about
20 people that was a significant number. I remember
her laughing and saying "Yep. One-a-month. Uh-huh,
one-a-month." This 'revolving door' concept became
fairly consistent throughout my early years at the three
station cluster. And that explains why my father heard
the announcements, I heard that the positions were filled,
and then there they were on the air again just 90-days
later. They were hiring 3 people at a time, only to have
the "One-A-Month" phenomena continue.

One sarcastic small agency owner used to call in, laughing over the phone: "They can't keep anybody in the seats!! THAT ought to tell- ya SOMETHING! Aaaaaah HA HA HA HA HA HAAAA!!!"

What we later learned was that the group of investors who had owned the stations just prior to a family-owned buyer taking over, were in so far over their heads with debt that they were literally giving the station's air time away to produce revenue, ANY revenue. In walked we "innocents", handed a price list that was twice what the advertisers had been paying, although a fair price for the quality of our "products and services", only to get the full force of the wrath of the current clients as they discovered that the new owners had doubled their rates overnight. The family-owned business, whom I'll call "Great Dane Media", complete with a logo of a huge dog on their letterhead, were a fairly successful group of operators with about 17 stations scattered in various markets in the northeast, mostly in Pennsylvania and upstate New York. Try starting a brand new career up against that kind of "headwind!"

THE "LIST"

I soon discovered that one of the "norms" in the radio business was that each new hire was handed a "list" of accounts, limited to around 60 since they reasoned that was all one person could adequately handle, given the limitations of time during the week. It was only when that I started calling to introduce myself to my "list" that I discovered that these were not real accounts. Instead they were nothing more than company names, phone numbers, contact persons that someone on the other side of the revolving door had once "claimed" so as to protect them from being called on by another salesperson. They were definitely not current customers or even previous customers or what you'd call 'billing accounts" just a "list' of names that were constantly regurgitated as each succeeding new hire was handed them. They had absolutely the same value as a business selected at random out of a telephone book. By the time I realized this, shifted my focus on going after and developing my own set of prospects from the bottom up that I realized my "list" had cost me about two months of wasted time. The company was simply "throwing bodies" against this tide, hoping against hope that THIS time things would be different. And it never was. There's that old definition of "insanity" tapping on our shoulder once again!

Once I started to develop my own, fresh, "list" did I immediately begin to see some success, and it came rather quickly for me. I immediately saw the value of live, local, on air personalities and the loyal following of listeners they were building. I soon embraced what was called the "live read" or the personal endorsement of a product or service by a trusted voice, someone that the listeners got to know on a personal basis from hearing their "show' each day, and someone whom they trusted when the host sang the praises of a particular business. Compared to a booming, fake-enthusiastic, "announcer's radio voice, these mainly unscripted, speaking-from-the-heart endorsements were infinitely more powerful and effective in causing the audience to believe what they heard and to act on these recommendations to visit the particular advertiser's business.

That's when I met a real talent I'll call Mike O'Leary. Mike was told to be the 'bad boy' of the line up and to become a "lightning rod" of controversy. He sounded a lot like Rush Limbaugh and like the popular talk show icon the principle basically held that: "Those who love him listen to him for about an hour per day; those who hate him listen for about TWO hours per day." Both men, in the end, are there for the entertainment value, interacting with, often arguing with an insulting their callers---who loved every minute of it!

UNRELENTING SUCCESS WITH LIVE AND LOCAL ON AIR PERSONALITIES

To briefly touch on any of the negativity of the situation, you have to admit that any business relationship that starts out on the basis of a blatant lie (The infamous "list", as one example) has nowhere to go but down. But I had been in sales for a number of years and realized that my success or failure was ultimately to be determined by my own efforts. And since the relentless pursuit of new business was both my forte' as well as my passion I set out to succeed. I teamed up with Mike O'Leary and we tore though the market, arranging long-term, mostly annual business with food manufacturers, moving companies, air purification inventors, custom woodworking craftsmen, heating and air conditioning specialists, and almost every other category of advertiser you can imagine. With Mike alone I sold 11 annual contracts, 7 of which were running at the same time. Mike had started at about the same time as I did so when I arrived there were no live endorsements going on at all. By 18 months into this "run" so many people had heard these endorsements that the calls started pouring in by other categories looking to take advantage of Mike's services. His $75,000 base salary soon ballooned to over $100,000 when you added in all his monthly talent fees, which were around $500 per month per advertiser!

There was one food manufacturer, Delinski's products who utilized two of our live, local air talents. We had an extremely popular "legendary" personality, "Uncle Dennis" Day, I'll call him, and a mid-morning lady I'll call Mary Likes. Delinski's used Mike and his booming voice in the afternoon for the unbridled enthusiasm he yelled into the studio microphone and Mary in the morning, who took a much softer approach, targeting to the ladies in the audience where she suggested various recipes as to how to prepare Delinski's main product, a chicken sausage line of various flavors that tasted like a seasoned pork product but was made entirely of chicken, and thus very heart and cholesterol-friendly. It was one of the most successful radio campaigns in the region at the time and the increase in volume forced the local supermarket chain to bring in hundred of pallets of product and actually inventory them in their warehouse whereas they had previously only spot purchased the line as needed.

All of this underscored a main strength of radio previous to the coming Telecommunications act of 1996—the use of live, local, recognizable on air personalities. In addition to their success as endorsers they were able to talk about local concerts, events, breaking local news and everything else going on locally that made the listener feel that they were being addressed by someone they personally knew. This was sort of a jump-starting of the most powerful form of advertising that, of course, being "word of mouth." I continued leading the field in new direct business as opposed to advertising agency "buys" that they called "purely transactional business." The later consisted of "an avail" which simply meant that an agency would call up looking for a "buy" for a particular demographic cell, i.e. "Women 25-54" and then began to beat up the poor salesperson on the other end of the line for a greatly reduced rate. All radio stations so value the "direct" business over the "transactional" business that they generally pay a commission rate about twice the percentage for direct as they do for the transactional. Part of this reason is that an agency immediately receives a 15% discount that they called "net' rates as opposed to 'gross' rates (before the discount) for their services. The determination as to which station gets 'on the buy' was, of course, determined by figures and rating points from---you guessed it---data obtained from the Arbitron diaries. Our immediate sales manager from our news/talk station often called it "ratings point efficiency" as opposed to "overall effectiveness" of the campaign. Some agencies were aware of this reality and I've met some of the finest people in the business who worked with me at agencies but the majority of them were basically wearing blinders and kneeling at the unreliable, statistically invalid 'altar' of the Arbitron ratings system in making their choices of stations.

THE 'HOLY GRAIL' OF "25-54"

Since I was dealing almost exclusively with direct accounts who were enjoying tremendous success I was able to avoid most of this agency tunnel vision but from time to time

I had to deal with it since a direct account would often engage the services of a full service agency who could buy TV, print, radio, billboards, and wide host of services.

The 25-54 "mantra" I felt then, and feel even stronger about now that the population continues to age, is utter nonsense when you read any statistical report on the population's wealth or buying habits. ANY government study will tell you that "80% of the nation's wealth is controlled by folks 50 years old and over." Doesn't this make logical sense to you? Someone 50 years old is likely earning much more than someone 25. If they had their first mortgage at 25 then 30 years later then, the 55-year old, had paid it off and had 100% equity. Their savings, 401-K, and all other investments would have had 30 years to build up. Their "net worth" and disposable income was light years beyond that of their 25-year old children! And yet, according to the folks with the blinders on, several things must happen when you turn 55 years old.

1. Your credit cards are cut up and your credit rating is automatically destroyed.
2. The equity in your home is somehow, magically removed from you.
3. Your savings and investments are taken from you as you bank accounts are drained and your 401-K and/or pensions disappear
4. All your worldly possessions are taken from you.
5. And you're thrown in your underwear, into the streets, homeless, destitute, and definitely someone who doesn't buy anything any more!

And yet the "25-54" dementia continues to exist, even 15 yeas later, even with the life expectancy nearly doubling since 1900. One manager used to say: "25-54" isn't a demographic, it's a family reunion!!"

This almost "militant ignorance" used to piss me off in 1995 when our station, average age 51, was left off so many different "buys" since the agencies were going after "25-54." It EXTREMELY pisses me off today!!

We're still in 1995-1996 for chronological purity of this book but today, as we approach the end of the first decade of the 21st century the cold hard facts are that the fastest growing demographic group of people coming to use the Internet is, believe it or not, those individuals 65+. Yet, in the world of "negative selling" where rival radio stations could only sell their stations by bashing the competition (always a loser's ploy in the end—negativity always has been) we would constantly hear "WFZ? They're too old, they don't have any money, and they don't buy anything!!!" Well friends I'd like to invite you to Vegas, on any luxury cruise, any European vacation, or onto the car lots of the Lexus, Cadillac, Mercedes, to the beachfront condos, to the high-end jewelry stores, and sit there for an hour and see who walks in and guess their age groups!

I once "closed" a deal with the biggest Ford dealership in Albany, New York, a place called ORANGE MOTORS. They had been selling cars since 1911 and were thus inundated by every sales rep in the region. The V.P. a nice gentleman named Jimmy Hollender, had obviously been brainwashed by dozens of '25-54' station reps. When I walked in he repeated, as if it was a subconscious, brainwashed, suggestion, planted in his mind: "OH, your station is too old!!" I answered "Jim, we represent the largest financial lending institution in the United

States of America!" As poor Jimmy grabbed a pen and paper and readied himself to write down the name of this magical bank, I stopped him and said, simply:

"The bank of mom and dad…" Jimmy gazed out into his own showroom and there, sitting at several sales cubicles, were indeed some 22 or 26-year old buyers---but each and every one of them was accompanied by "Mom", "Dad" or often BOTH of them—either writing out a check for the down payment on the $32,000 mustang, if not actually cosigning for the loan. Jimmy signed an annual agreement a few moments later. Reality has a way of 'getting through' the bull crap and ignorance eventually.

THE LOWLIFE, UNRESPECTED SALES PERSON

A phenomena that I had experienced earlier in wholesale foodservice sales and that seemed to be one of the ruling principles in radio sales as well was the "lifeblood "of the business, the people who actually made the sales that produced the income that paid the bills and hence the salaries of all of the managers, production people operations managers, the spot traffic department, the promotions people, the sales secretaries, and everyone else receiving an income---were treated as the lowest form of life on the planet. Again this is not a universal truth. I only held 4 different radio sales positions in my life and I'm simply talking about one of them, my experience at WFZ in Schenectady New York with Great Dane media in the mid to late 1990's.

But during my tenure there the sad reality was that almost everyone, from the operations manager to the promotions director to the studio and production people, right down to the sales management, even to "little Mike" a gofer running errands for the on-air personalities, as well as all of the 'sales support' folks looked down and talked down to the sales people as if they were pure garbage, a necessary evil that they somehow had to put up with, yet despise with all of their hearts. As national talk show host, Mr. Neal Bortz once put it, referring to another matter: "What kind of MORONIC IMBECILITY does THAT take?!!!" Here is just a sampling of a few of the "characters" that illustrate this point.

A. Don Larker, operations manager: "I'm sick of hearing that the salespeople pay our salary!! That's bullshit! They sell OUR products!!!" True, Don. We do sell your products. We sell them to our advertisers who in turn write the checks that go into the company's bank account out of which you and everyone else gets paid. Follow your reasoning all of the way to the end and you'll see how foolish a statement that is. Don was an egotistical, former DJ who talked in a loud, resonant "on air voice" even when in a normal conversation, who thought so much of himself it was incredible. He couldn't sell his way out of a condom. But he somehow he felt 'superior' to the lowly sales staff and talked down to them accordingly.

B. Larry Gronski: Sales manager who would have fit into the "Nero" of Rome role, who reportedly 'fiddled while Rome burned' and was incapable of handling or solving an internal problem head on. Deathly fearing any conflict, he was truly a nice and decent gentleman but in his mind there was no such thing as a 'problem' only a "challenge." He took having a "positive attitude" to extremes. If someone had rushed up and told him: "Larry, your entire family just got run over and killed by a train but we were able to save your little cat, 'kitty-shoes'!!" he would have thrust his arm confidently up into the air and said, with a smile: "Well THAT'S positive!!"

C. Diana Shank: Our promotions director who was completely devoid of any personality or people skills whatsoever—perfect qualities in a promotions director. You'd walk by her in the halls and say "good morning, Diana!" and she'd answer by rudely pushing you aside and saying "excuse me!" in response. Attempting to execute any promotional idea was thus nearly impossible. She slurred her words together, prompting one sales person to remark: "You'd think that if you truly wanted to be 'in radio' that you'd take a little more time with your enunciation and your elocution of your speaking style!"

D. Michael Warren—Another 'positive' guy, and head V.P and general manager of all 3 stations, he'd listen to motivational tapes, and then internalize them so much that the next day he'd jump up on the conference table in the midst of a sales meeting and yell: "Everybody's got a little bag of shit that they're carrying around here! We've got to get it out and air it all out to get rid of it!!" This was motivation? It was also met with total shock from a completely frozen audience of about 20 seated sales people around the table had no clue as to what he was talking about.

E. "Carol the sales secretary" who made a contorted face whenever someone asked her to do her job and assemble a proposal and spent about 50% of he time hiding in the ladies room.

F. Neal Lutz: The 'studio producer' who was at constant odds with, and continuously insulting to the sales staff as they handed in commercial copy and he began to fight each one, tooth and nail, about the way things were phrased, or something ran too long or was off message. Now was it Neal who was out in the field getting to know what messages the potential or current customers wanted to convey? Or was it the poor sales staff, continuously batted like a tennis ball, back and forth between the paying customer's demands and the "sales support" team inside the building? One sales rep's mantra was that "someone ought to explain to some of these people the meaning of 'SALES SUPPORT.!!' Another rep ran up to Larry one day and said, in a pleading, almost whimpering voice: "Larry! There's no support! There's no support!!" I believe Larry' answer, as he thrust his forearm upward into the air was something like: "THAT"S positive!!"

G. Sally Mettier, the business manager, who, knew full well that if an invoice wasn't paid within 90 days the salesperson would lose their commission. Somehow, some way, she mysteriously ran out of stamps and the postage meter ran dry for weeks at a time at the end of each month. We discovered that Sally had arranged a side deal where she would get an override for a percentage of every "unpaid" or charge-back on all previously paid sales commissions. The end of the month was when the bills and invoices were to go out. Even the advertisers themselves, many of whom even loudly complained when we had them in for "focus groups" on how we could improve our service, complained that they'd really appreciate receiving their bills on timely basis. They couldn't understand the 30-40 days delay. Their unwitting accounts payable departments normally paid their bills within 60-days. But receiving their statements 30-40 days late resulted in this delayed cycle naturally causing our accounts receivables to go "over 90" thus illegally and immorally burning the sales people out of their commissions on a regular basis. Yes, it seems as if 'GREAT DANE MEDIA' had once again 'LIFTED ITS LEG' upon the poor saps on the sales force!!!! This is a legitimate business?!! Maybe for Bernie Madoff!!

There were at least a half-dozen more "support" personnel with the same attitude and to show that there is indeed a thing called "Karma" in this world and to illustrate this point I will tell you that, by the time I moved out of the state to take a better position in Florida, or shortly after, EVERY SINGLE ONE OF THESE PEOPLE HAD BEEN FIRED OR OTHERWISE ELIMINATED!! EVERY LAST ONE OF THEM!!!

This next phenomena is one that I witnessed previously in sales and since my experience at WFZ has grown exponentially worse in the industry.

First, a sales person is hired after rigorous background and resume' examinations, countless interviews with 'trick' questions to prove that they're a self-motivated, enterprising, aggressive selling, time-management expertise, well-prepared professional sales personal with unbounded people and sales skills and determination to succeed and excel at their job.

Second, someone way up the "chain of command" usually some totally blank of a personality 'bean-counter' who couldn't sell his or her way out of a…well, you know, needs to see some sales numbers to pay the bills and show a profit for the bankers, financiers, stock holders, or owners "comes down" on the upper layers of management to "make their goals" (read "quotas", a real "goal' is something that comes from within, not something imposed on you by someone else.). There the 'threat' begins.

Third, the various layers of management begin to intimidate each lower stratum, to hit these "numbers" be they realistic or not.

Fourth, the management closest to the sales force begins to intimidate or threaten the sales force. Doesn't anybody realize that these sales people WANT to sell as much as they possibly can? Don't they think that these folks have bills to pay, families to feed? Is the language of the threat really productive, does the cattle-prod really have to be jammed into the lifeblood?!! My take is that there HAS to be a more productive way to run a business than everyone at every level looking over their shoulder and 'covering their ass?' Isn't there a more efficient means of motivation that utter nonsense like that?!!

And the old definition of insanity again comes calling as the revolving door continues to spin so fast that it almost takes the whole building off the ground!

They once brought in a national "motivational speaker" named Don Bevridge, who bragged that he was such a "pull yourself up by your own bootstraps' type of guy that when his 18 year old son asked for some money to attend college Don immediate threw him right out of the house and into the streets so the kid would 'get tough' and 'learn the hard way' like his dad had to. At one point in his speech, during a phrase that every salesperson relished forever, Don pounded the podium as he spoke these words, the whole room echoing loudly since the sound system greatly magnified his pounding as well as his words:

"…..and I'll tellya something else too!! Whenever management feels that it has to play policeman….you are ON YOUR WAY OUT OF BUSINESS!!!!" A loud cheer went up from the sales audience, although our managers later tried to play down that statement by saying: "well, we didn't agree wit EVERYTHING he said."

At one point in 1995, as I was attempting to sell a start-up Internet company they were simultaneously trying to sell our company on using the Internet as a revenue generating tool. They came in, clumsily attempted several times then finally accessed the primitive "Net" then left. After their presentation I asked Larry what he thought. He shook his head 'no' and I asked: "What? You don't see any future application for it?" He replied "No, not really." My technological skills are still very limited but at least I can state, from a historical perspective, that I had been the one to introduce the Internet to the company. And this was a company that was destined to be a part of one of the largest 'consolidators' in the entire radio industry several years later; just a little historical footnote here.

I continued to out perform all of the sales people at all 3 radio stations because I kept my head down and continued to open new business, new DIRECT business, like nobody before or after my 1994-1996 initial run at WFZ news/talk radio in Schenectady. I also learned from the masters. We often had various management and visiting experts and teachers who taught us how we could use radio to create "theme" programs that used to dramatically differentiate myself from the competition. I did a series called "Allergy Answers" for a huge Allergy medical group, "Chiropracticalities" for a Spine practice, "Word-of-Mouth" for dental conglomerates, and "Matters of the Heart" for a huge cardiology practice. I used the "informational" nature of the news/talk format to elevate the normal 60-second commercial to a series of medical and educational vignettes, taking these messages up a notch from the normal "yelling in your face" delivery of say, a car commercial. It worked again and again. I also learned the value of radio as an employee recruitment tool and began to make a fortune from radio recruiting, opening up a whole new universe of advertising categories within the human resources field with a scientifically-designed and implemented radio recruitment program. Who would use radio to search for a nuclear physicist, with a top-security government clearance—a true "needle in a haystack" How about General Dynamics?! This was

NOT your normal advertiser, but a new account. This was a 100% previously untapped source of radio revenue and I rode it all the way to the bank.

Then, in late 1996, as The Telecommunications act began to create huge radio consolidation groups, my phone rang from an out of state call………..

CHAPTER FOUR

MY FIRST EXPERIENCE WITH THE WORLD OF 'RADIO CONSOLODATION' AND ITS DETREMENTIAL EFFECT ON HUMAN BEINGS OF ANY KIND

After almost two years of unbridled and ever-growing success despite working in market that was truly dying everywhere one looked, I received a very strange phone call from a woman in northeast Pennsylvania, around the Scranton area.

A consolidator called "Synair Communications" was looking for a unique individual to move to Scranton and take over a huge "list" (there's the deadly word again) of accounts from a top sales producer who was being promoted to sales manager. According to the woman on the phone I had been recommended by many of my radio peers and salespeople in the Albany-Schenectady-

Troy "metro" region as the best candidate for this position. The sales position entailed taking over a 'list" that was currently producing about $70,000 per month in revenue for "Synair Broadcasting." That, being a mix of direct and agency business was akin to somewhere around a $120,000 per year in income.

Naturally I had a few questions.

First, who exactly was recommending me for this lucrative sales job and why hadn't that person taken the opportunity themselves? The woman, "Linda" answered that she wasn't allowed to tell me but that the answer to the second part of the question was that all of my "supporters" were entrenched in the "Capital District" as they called my region, with various school, civic, job, and other commitments and couldn't relocate at that time. This would mean moving to a smaller market which went against the grain of my past experience. I had done much better by moving to a much larger market(Los Angeles in the foodservice business in the 1980's) where my new account development skills worked well since there was a much larger 'candy store' to play in and unlimited opportunities just due to the sheer volume of available businesses to approach. However, I thought that a very high income coupled with a more rural, less hectic market, just might be the ideal combination. So I went for the interview, was offered the job, and left WFZ in Schenectady on good terms with my disappointed manager saying that he didn't want to hold me back if I had indeed a much more lucrative opportunity. I had performed so well that they told me that my 'desk would always be open' should I decide to return.

Being a single guy I threw my socks and underwear in the back of my car and moved the 100-mile, 2-hours to the Scranton Pennsylvania area.

What I'm about to tell you will sound like a complete fabrication, if not at least a wild exaggeration but I swear and can prove that it is absolutely 100% accurate.

I arrived in northeastern Pennsylvania in the late spring of 1996 and was immediately sent out to get the feel of the market and to open some new business. I didn't immediately ask about this new, huge, block of business since I knew for sure that it was in the works and I had a substantial 6-month guaranteed salary which easily took care of all of my moving and expenses.

Not long after my arrival I began to see instances of how 'Synair' was treating their employees. I overheard one new hire outside, almost in tears, yelling to some fellow employee: "Where does he get off in telling me 'DON'T COME BACK WITHOUT AN ORDER!??"I thought it to be kind of a cruel thing for a boss to say, since, in every transaction there are at least TWO individuals involved; the salesperson, doing their best to develop new business and that "other" entity, the person they were trying to sell. The salesperson can be putting out maximum effort and have all of the tools and skills in the world. But if the prospect doesn't 'get it', doesn't want to 'get it' or for whatever reason isn't ready to buy then all the rep can do is to 'go onto the next one' and start all over again. Just to pose an obvious question but what happens when the "next one" is just as much of a roadblock, for whatever reason, as the "last one?" I guess what I'm saying is that 'it takes two to tango' and you can have the finest sales professional in the world, targeting the perfect potential account for the particular station but you're always going into the unknown. You haven't known that person all their lives since you just met. You're not their mother and/or their father, you weren't the one who brought them up, instilled whatever value system or morals they may have, you didn't teach them about honesty, right from wrong, or how to behave. The salesperson's success, therefore, is at least a function of who they're dealing with. And there is an entire universe of things out there that are simply and totally beyond your control.

But not to the upper management or owners; you're supposed to be 100% responsible and be able to answer for the words, actions, behavior, promises, and quality of character of each and every person you interact with. I overheard and have been in the middle of conversations that took the form of: "…but he said that he was going to…and you told us that he was going to…..and you were certain that they were going to….." etc. But you can never be. As one gal later in my career put it: "I'm NOT inside my customer's head!! They think I'm inside my customer's head!!!" That was the best way of describing it I've ever heard!!

But when the" you-know-what" runs downhill it doesn't matter. There's always someone, in terror, looking over their shoulder, answering to some higher-up, mumbling out what THEY think their SALESPEOPLE think of a completely unknown personality or entity. I've seen charts and graphs and absolutely inane questions such as "Are you 80% sure it's going to close?!! Are you 40% sure?!!" I finally came up with my own formula.

Take the percentage of how much I'm sure, multiply that by the quality of the character and honesty of the person telling me that they're going to do one thing or the other and the final net figure of that multiplication is my "net sureness" of what will happen. The 'character and honesty' figure is always an unknown. I didn't bring them up, I'm didn't instill in them their values, honesty, etc. etc.

But let's leave the greatest and most incredible part of this story for the last. For one, while I was there at Synair I happened to meet a real snake called "Rughead" Mike Remeedy. The 'Rughead' part came from the fact that he had such an obvious wig that it looked like he was wearing a helmet. He was one of the managers of another station in the cluster who was telling the salespeople: 'Don't come back without an order!!' He also monitored my station, heard of an advertiser, and then went out bad-mouthed his own sister station, (mine) stealing the account from me with totally negative selling and a cacophony of lies and misinterpretations about my station. This 'grab-grab-take-take-me-me-mine-mine' phenomenon was to be a hallmark of one of the things I thought was the true underbelly of societal evolution in the radio industry.

But the absolute worst part was that everything that the 'recruiter' Linda had been telling all of the new hires was a 100% lie. Synair couldn't recruit salespeople in the immediate area since they all had non-compete clauses in their sales employment contracts. So they set this woman up to call all over the northeast and Midwest with the same story about the huge "$70,000 list" that was just waiting for them to assume.

It was a lie; a blatant lie repeated over and over again to dozens and dozens of poor saps. These unfortunate individuals had sold their houses all over the northeast and Mid-Atlantic states, bought homes in the Scranton area, moved their screaming, crying children out of their schools and away from their lifelong friends, left behind their own circles of friends and family, civic and social organizational frameworks---all to 'follow the yellow brick road' right to hell in a no man's land of a small, poor market, where they were then stuck! As the light began to go on I could see that one week there were 10 reps at our station, the next week nine, then eight, seven, six—as each person discovered that they and been lied to and completely duped into believing that "you were recommended as the best candidate!!"

It was one of the lowest, most immoral acts that I've ever personally witnessed a whole organization pull off. And it literally destroyed dozens and dozens of people's lives!! In the meantime I was doing my usual thing, opening up a bunch of new business, including one of the biggest auto dealers in the entire state of Pennsylvania, a dealership called 'Cocia Ford" who had never even done radio and never intended to…but did so with me. I received my usual awards, nailed records, and accolades, and since my desk back in Schenectady was 'always open' and since my old company was continuously calling me and offering me my old position back, I finally left and drove the two hours back to Schenectady and resumed my old job.

I don't know what happened to all of the poor bastards who didn't have that luxury or liquidity, but the individuals and corporate snakes that pulled off this farce on them will someday, if indeed there is justice in the world, "get theirs!" And it is my sincerest hope that they 'get theirs' with the full force of both the good Lord's and the universe's complete retribution and punishment to the ultimate extent of nature's fury!!!

Just for kicks, a few years later I did some market research, and "Synair" had completely self-destructed in that market and was no longer in business there. "As ye sow so shall ye reap" according to the Book of Proverbs. I like the more modern expression of "WHAT GO AROUND COME AROUND Y'KNOW WHAT'AM SAYIN?!!! Welcome to the world of radio consolidation!!!!

A radio sale, like most other sales situations is not rocket science. It's simply a game of numbers. Only about 4% of people are ready to buy today. So my success was mainly the ability to make between 50 and 100 sales attempts per day. This could take the form of phone calls, e-mails, and 'seed' or approach letters. If you made the 300-500 attempts per week you would generally succeed. And remember that so many of these people have been burned before in some sales situation that they have their guard up. They simply don't trust you. You're always and continuously walking in the footsteps of someone who was told "Don't come back without a sale!" They've heard: "we're number one!" They've been sold a "package" by a hit and run "sales reptile" as Dr. LeNoble used to call them; someone who would tell the prospect anything the potential client wanted to ear just to get a sale. So you're frequently told: "I tried radio once and it didn't work!" Radio like any other media is a frequency medium. It goes back to the old schoolhouses on the prairie in the late 1,800's when the teacher's by accident, discovered that it took 3 repetitions before a particular lesson 'sank in' to the student's mind. And this has been the basis of all advertising ever since.

It's especially true in today's world, where each of us is bombarded by 2,000 to 3,000 'sales messages per day' in our daily lives. You awake to write something down. On the pen there's an advertisement for something, catch the morning news on radio and TV and there they come again. Drive to work past 500 signs and billboards, each trying to 'sell you something' Stop into your local supermarket and while walking the isles 1,000 displays, signs, voices over the loudspeaker in the store radio are all "selling." On your drive home it continues with the signs and billboards, sit in front of the TV at night and it just keeps s going on, drift off to sleep with your radio and it never stops. The 3 repetitions is thus a bare minimum since you have to get through all of the 'clutter' of the normal day to have a message, finally 'sink in" and then it has to "sink in" to that 4% who are immediately ready to act on it. An extremely small percentage of individuals are mentally ready to separate "concept" rejection (your sales message) from "personal" rejection (you, the individual) and to do it day after day, being 'rejected' 98 out of 100 times. Dr LeNoble has identified 4 main reasons why "radio doesn't work."

1. You buy what station you personally like rather than one that best fits your target customer. You're 'shootin' over there while the target's over here!" according to the good doctor.

2. The 'two-week Syndrome." If you went to the gym and started a work out program you'd see

some sort of results in two weeks, but not much. And yet some folks actually think that they can "try radio" instead of utilize radio the right way with continuous repetition. The 4% of THEIR customers cannot usually be reached in just two weeks. It's a small little dot on the page that grows larger as a universe as some 'triggering mechanism' or event in one's life suddenly causes them to want to buy or to take action. Two weeks is approximately 4% of the total year's time you're in business. You can't expect miracles in two weeks; the numbers are just not on your side. If not continuously reinforced, according to LeNoble and other studies, 75% of a message is forgotten in two weeks and 95% is gone out of the mind within 3-weeks time.

3. The "Spray and pray phenomenon." So many people take their budget and completely dilute it by thinking that they have to do "a little radio" "a little TV", "let's not forget direct mail'. 'We better cover the newspaper too" and thus they fail to dominate one group of individuals with sufficient repeated impressions and blame the next "Ronnie radio" who walks in the door. Larry used to repeat that it's not how many different individuals you reach as much as it is in reaching that same individual with repeated impressions. "Spraying and praying" may reach more people. But it's wasted money since you fail to reach the same individual with repeated impressions.

4. Fraud, Slam Dunk. Many of these 'consolidators' like Synair, bought their stations at greatly inflated

prices as a function of their annual income, in 1995-1996 it was usually a multiple of around 15 times annual revenue = price of station. Today, after they wrecked the business in ways you'll soon see it's barely 3 or 4 times' annual revenue. Hence came the 'don't come back without a sale" threat which just resulted in a poorly executed message or commercial, thrown together without sufficient planning or partnership with the client, and naturally the results were disappointing.

The basic downfall of radio began with the consolidators "taking their eye off the ball." To please the bankers, financiers, stockholders, and thus their bottom line they completely ignored what they had all stated were their main 3 groups of customers:

A. Their advertisers, with 'slam dunk" inadequately produced and delivered products and campaigns, just to "don't come back without a sale!"

B. Their listeners, who they disserved, with voice-tracking in advance to "save money" as during that hurricane situation in the first chapter and other ways of 'doing it on the cheap.'

C. Their employees, especially the sales force, the lifeblood who they threatened, intimidated, and fired in huge an ever-increasing numbers. Always thinking that the next person to occupy the seat would somehow be a savior, descending from the clouds who would magically turn the situation around but who just became yet another rider of the revolving door due to the same, totally inane, business model. INSANITY, INSANITY, AND MORE INSANITY!

In any case I returned to Schenectady where I once again led the field in new direct business, building and learning from my own mistakes as well as from some of the aforementioned "masters" of the business. And during my last full year there in 1998, I received an award that said that out of 27 total salespeople in three radio stations I was one out only 3 who achieved my annual goal. Theme programs with an interwoven title, like "Matters of the Heart" and Radio recruiting to uncover brand new revenue streams put me over the top.

But enough about me for the moment. How about society as a whole? How about the people we had to deal with on a daily basis. Have we somehow been 'dumbed down' as a society over the years? Has our government run educational system produced an ever less grounded social "product?" Please read on........

CHAPTER FIVE

HAVE WE ALL INDEED, BEEN "DUMBED DOWN? OVER THE YEARS?

Recently the Russian state newspaper, "Pravda" which means "Truth" in the Russian language, ran an article that is shocking to most American readers.

It addressed, amongst other things, that the American government-run school system, has systematically watered-down, or devalued the American schools educational system, precisely to produce an uneducated populace, ripe for takeover. We've all witnessed the phenomena of watered down courses in the students' history books; i.e. George Washington was a racist Indian Killer, who kept slaves and now onto chapter two…

I'm exaggerating of course but the facts are there. Recent reports tell us that fully 40% of Americans cannot name the three branches of the U.S. government. That alone is disturbing enough. But psychologists, educators and even motivational speakers have been talking about this issue for decades.

The 'dean of personal development', Earl Nightingale, once said that "we sometimes get the impression that most people TIPTOE through life…in order to make it safely….to death!"

And perhaps it's not all our own fault or that of 'the government.' In today's hectic, two-parent working family, with technology accelerating so rapidly, it's not hard to believe. Between 1900 and 1920, for example, the entire sum of the world's knowledge doubled. It took 20 years for this to happen. Today, with the Internet and the rapid globalization and pace of invention the whole of the world's knowledge is doubling approximately every 6-months! That naturally has to leave most of us behind, and falling further and further behind all of the time.

But I've noticed a trend in the prospects I've interacted with in the radio business. So many folks are literally running scared these days. They indeed 'tiptoe' through their daily existence, afraid to make a decision for fear that if they decide wrong they will suffer grave consequences. Many seem totally disconnected from life going on around them. They go to work like automatons, push their pencils or tap their computers, not really relishing what they do or even really enjoying it let alone being invigorated by it. They think constantly of 'the weekend' when they can 'kick back and relax' from the constant stresses of daily reality. They're afraid to make a decision, they're afraid to step out of their own little comfort zones. And so taking a stand or 'stepping up to the plate' so to speak, to implement an advertising campaign is something they truly fear.

Noted psychologist, and motivational speaker, Dr. Wayne Dyer, has said that "the HEIGHT of ignorance is in rejecting something you know nothing about!" And yet I've witnessed this happen time and time again. It's almost like a blatant, militant ignorance that permeates the whole society. Thus potential advertisers will often recoil in fear and dread when asked to make a decision on where and how to advertise. I believe that this is directly related to this 'numbing down' of the entire society, where we go scurrying like small animals into a cave in fear of a perceived threat, often one that, once fully examined, is no threat at all. THIS is what radio or any other kind of salespeople face every day; fear, paralyzing inaction, rejection of the unknown, "playing it safe" 'getting through the week where our lives are supposed to manifest to that blessed 'weekend' where the whole wicked world goes away, only to return on Monday. This partially explains why, according to the American medical Association, most heart attacks occur on Monday mornings. This is when that cruel, merciless world reappears, and, in the case of the potential advertiser, once again frightening decisions have to be faced.

Examining this 'dumb-down' idea myself, I once asked two 'twenty-something' girls who were part-time college students, working their way through school while bartending at a local family restaurant a recent history question. I asked them: "Can either of you name the famous American who uttered the following words?" And as I asked I shook my head slightly from side to side and purposely spoke in a slightly hoarse voice, doing my best imitation of "The gipper" president Ronald Wilson Reagan: "Mr. Gorbachev.....TEAR DOWN THIS

WALL!!!" They looked at each other, completely puzzled and then both looked back at me and said 'no. that's that?' I told them that it was "Snoop Dog" speaking at the beginning of his latest rap album. The fall of Communism? The ending of the cold war?!! No clue from either one!!

Are we really "dumbed-down?" What follows is an actual eighth grade final exam from the Kansas school system from 1895, courtesy of the Kansas Salina Journal. I wonder how many 4-year college graduates could pass this test today without the aid of calculators or the Internet. This is true, it's factual, and it should scare the living hell out of you!!

WHAT IT TOOK TO GET AN 8TH GRADE EDUCATION IN 1895...

Remember when grandparents and great-grandparents stated that they only had an 8th grade education? Well, check this out. Could any of us have passed the 8th grade in 1895?

This is the eighth-grade final exam from 1895 in Salina, Kansas, USA. It was taken from the original document on file at the Smokey Valley Genealogical Society and Library in Salina, and reprinted by the Salina Journal.

8th Grade Final Exam: Salina , KS - 1895

Grammar (Time, one hour)

1. Give nine rules for the use of capital letters.

2.. Name the parts of speech and define those that have no modifications.

3. Define verse, stanza and paragraph

4. What are the principal parts of a verb? Give principal parts of 'lie, 'play,' and 'run.'

5. Define case; illustrate each case.

6 What is punctuation? Give rules for principal marks of punctuation..

7 - 10. Write a composition of about 150 words and show therein that you understand the practical use of the rules of grammar.

Arithmetic (Time,1 hour 15 minutes)

1. Name and define the Fundamental Rules of Arithmetic.

2. A wagon box is 2 ft. Deep, 10 feet long, and 3 ft. Wide. How many bushels of wheat will it hold?

3. If a load of wheat weighs 3,942 lbs., what is it worth at 50cts/bushel, deducting 1,050 lbs.. For tare?

4. District No 33 has a valuation of $35,000... What is the necessary levy to carry on a school seven months at $50 per month, and have $104 for incidentals?

5. Find the cost of 6,720 lbs. Coal at $6.00 per ton.

6. Find the interest of $512.60 for 8 months and 18 days at 7 percent.

7. What is the cost of 40 boards 12 inches wide and 16 ft.. Long at $20 per metre?

8. Find bank discount on $300 for 90 days (no grace) at 10 percent.

9. What is the cost of a square farm at $15 per acre, the distance of which is 640 rods?

10. Write a Bank Check, a Promissory Note, and a Receipt

U.S. History (Time, 45 minutes)

1. Give the epochs into which U.S. History is divided

2. Give an account of the discovery of America by Columbus

3. Relate the causes and results of the Revolutionary War.

4. Show the territorial growth of the United States

5.. Tell what you can of the history of Kansas

6. Describe three of the most prominent battles of the Rebellion.

7. Who were the following: Morse, Whitney, Fulton , Bell , Lincoln , Penn, and Howe?

8. Name events connected with the following dates: 1607, 1620, 1800, 1849, 1865.

Orthography (Time, one hour)
[Do we even know what this is??]

1. What is meant by the following: alphabet, phonetic, orthography, etymology, syllabication

2.. What are elementary sounds? How classified?

3. What are the following, and give examples of each: trigraph, sub vocals, diphthong, cognate letters, lingual.

4. Give four substitutes for caret 'u.' (HUH?)

5. Give two rules for spelling words with final 'e.' Name two exceptions under each rule.

6. Give two uses of silent letters in spelling. Illustrate each.

7. Define the following prefixes and use in connection with a word: bi, dis-mis, pre, semi, post, non, inter, mono, sup.

8.. Mark diacritically and divide into syllables the following, and name the sign that indicates the sound: card, ball, mercy, sir, odd, cell, rise, blood, fare, last.

9. Use the following correctly in sentences: cite, site, sight, fane, fain, feign, vane, vain, vein, raze, raise, rays.

10. Write 10 words frequently mispronounced and indicate pronunciation by use of diacritical marks and by syllabication.

Geography (Time, one hour)

1 What is climate? Upon what does climate depend?

2. How do you account for the extremes of climate in Kansas ?

3. Of what use are rivers? Of what use is the ocean?

4.. Describe the mountains of North America

5. Name and describe the following: Monrovia, Odessa , Denver , Manitoba , Hecla , Yukon , St. Helena, Juan Fernandez, Aspinwall and Orinoco

6. Name and locate the principal trade centers of the U.S. Name all the republics of Europe and give the capital of each.

8. Why is the Atlantic Coast colder than the Pacific in the same latitude?

9.. Describe the process by which the water of the ocean returns to the sources of rivers.

10. Describe the movements of the earth. Give the inclination of the earth.

Notice that the exam took FIVE HOURS to complete.

Gives the saying 'he only had an 8th grade education' a whole new meaning, doesn't it?!

Also shows you how much our education system has changed.
NO, I don't have the answers.
YES, 20I don't know the answers to most of these questions.

CHAPTER SIX

ANOTHER JOURNEY INTO THE UNKNOWN AND MY INTERACTION WITH THE BIGGEST CONSOLODATOR GROUP OF THEM ALL

Back in the 'good old days" of radio in the late 1990's you were still able to arrange small trade deals for yourself or your company under certain circumstances. I received a trade bonus for hitting my first quarter 'goal" in 1999 and used it to book a two way flight to the Tampa Bay area, from Albany International airport, where I intended to speak to a huge news/talk station in the Brandon, Florida area. This station was one that sales manager Larry Gronski had spoken about many times and was also a part of the "Carrier Wave" group that was gobbling up station groups all over the country and was in the process of doing so in Florida. Poor Larry had been a recent victim, several times over, of radio takeovers, buyouts, and then consolidations. Management was the first thing that was replaced when a new corporation moved into a market to take over operations. Larry had been bounced around the country like he was part of the equipment from a Harlem Globetrotters tour.

I had met a tall Texan, the president of Carrier Wave recently whom I'll call "Lawrence Mayer." As he shook my hand a management voice introduced me by telling Mr. Mayer that "Bob is our non-spot revenue leader." "Non-Spot" included radio recruiting, manufacturer-funded programs through local advertisers, several print publications about the stations, cookbooks, almanacs, as well as revenue generated by the nascent Internet, by now, in 1999, very much a part of a trend I had predicted in 1995 when the people came in and first presented it to WFZ. "Carrier Wave" was now in negotiations to purchase the family-owned "Great Dane" media as part of Carrier's march to eventually own approximately 1,200 radio stations out of the approximately 11,400 total stations in the United States.

"Non-spot revenue?" Mr. Mayer drawled in his thick Texas accent, "That's my favorite subject!" Now, not 6 months later, in April of 1999 I was interviewing at one of his Florida properties, itself in the process of being acquired by Carrier Wave. I was working according to my old formula. I had left my position as a wholesale foodservice distributor salesman in the early 1980's, gone to none other than Los Angeles, California, and more than quadrupled my income and ended up with beachfront property. The larger market idea had been a successful model since I loved opening new business and "The Capital District" of Albany-Schenectady-Troy was a dying market. Schenectady, for example, was once a thriving factory town when General Electric was humming along in it's heyday in the 1940's and 1950's and "G.E." alone employed some 40,000 people in that region. Now, in the later 1990's, jobs and materials outsourced, the city was a ghost town, "G.E." had only around 3,500 daily workers reporting to its sprawling campus, and Schenectady, in spite of hosting several of the nation's highest quality college institutions, was little more than a ghost town. The main businesses were seedy bars, restaurants barely hanging on, and streetwalking prostitutes, gangs, and drug "shooting galleries." The weather was nothing short of hell on earth. We had two weeks of spring, two weeks of autumn, and the swiftest transition from freezing snowbound cold, to brutally hot, sweltering humid summers---hotter and more miserable than even in Florida. A friend of mine put it best when he complained: "We either freeze or sweat! We either freeze or we sweat! Nothing in-between!!" I joked that this region of the country, leading the U.S. in the number of people moving away (I believe North Carolina at the time had the distinction of the largest influx of new residents) was a nice place to be "from", as in 'AWAY-FROM!'

What finally blew me out the door from this area and on to Florida, however, were the cruel, insulting actions of yet two more "superstars" form the aforementioned line-up of salesperson-haters at WFZ. They were both woman who had been brought in from outside the business as "NTR managers". ("NTR" stood for non-traditional revenue and is the exact same as non-spot revenue just mentioned.) These two gals, one and then the other, thought nothing of yelling into the faces of the sales people and insulting them in front of their peers. Clueless to any people skills, they should have read that famous book by Dale Carnegie "How to win friends and influence people". They would have then at least had the basics. But they did not. They were so insulting that one 'took me to task' for actually calling on one of my own accounts, simply because she had a side agenda with an unsavory rep from one of our sister stations who was trying to sneak in a non-spot sale at the same time I happened to be there on a regular appointment. The second one, with the blessing of management, stood at one of our sales meetings and used a tactic that is guaranteed NOT to work with me---the language of the threat! She had come in and threatened the sales force at WFZ that if we didn't sell at least one sponsorship in our upcoming print publication (I was averaging 4 to 6 in each, and as just mentioned, leading the field, so it was not a threat I took personally, but as part of the sales 'team.') then we would lose an account. If another print publication came up and we didn't sell at least one then we'd lose a $10,000 account. The "punishment" would continue to accelerate after that!

I had already been interviewing in Florida and been offered a sales job, planning on leaving anyway so the threat rolled off me like water off a duck's back. But their previous insulting behavior had 'gotten' to me to the extent that I had endured sleepless nights, and introspective "Powerwalks" in which I was obsessed with just how I was going to tell them off-loud and dirty, and it was effecting my enjoyment of my job. I was primed for a move anyway and these final insults and threats simply validated, in my mind, my decision to 'walk' at the top of my game in the "Capital District' about 1,300 miles 'down the road.'

In any case, for the second time in my career at WFZ, I threw my belongings into my car and headed out on the 1,300-mile journey south to Florida. I was actually qualified to do so without actually "quitting" my job. When the "big boys" had visited 'Great Dane" prior to the buyout by "Carrier Wave" they asked the assembled staff if there were any questions. One question arose from somewhere in the crowd:

"Are there any relocation opportunities?" The "big boys" answered, almost sarcastically:

"Yes, we hear that a lot from people who want to get away from the ice and snow in the northeast, and yes, there ARE opportunities to relocate, assuming you've hit your annual goals here. We want the cream of the crop." They looked back and forth across the sea of faces and then followed up with:

"Any more questions? " I raised my hand. Remember I was only one out of 3 people from the 27 salespeople in the three-station group who had indeed hit my annual goal the year before and had the trophy to prove it. I still do. I was qualified to relocate.

"Relocate? Like where?" I asked.

"How about Tampa, Florida came the reply.

"Where do I sign?!!" I yelled back, without hesitation. The room erupted in waves of laughter. Little did they know!!!

ARRIVAL IN TAMPA BAY, "CARRIER WAVE COMMUNICATIONS" AND MY THREE

BUDGETS FROM: NEWS/TALK, SPOTS/ TALK AND MY 'SPORTS BUDGET."

It was repeated many times by many sales folks at Carrier Wave in Brandon Florida, a suburb of Tampa. No one at any of the other 5 stations in this new cluster of consolidators envied the fact that once sales force, out of the 6-station cluster and one of the biggest and first of the group of consolidators, was responsible for hitting 3 different on air radio budgets.

"WFLB"- The "B" standing for Brandon, was the news/talk leader in the region.

"WDAB-Was a small, sports/talk station whose main strength was in reaching men 25-54 and yet ranked 20th even in that, their strongest and 'target' demographic cell in the market since the signal as well as the audience was very small.

"The Sports Team" which will go unmentioned at this time, but ranked at the very bottom of the entire league in their sport, and was basically both new as well as the laughing stock of that particular sports profession in 1999 when I came aboard "Carrier Wave Communications" in May of that year.

As usual, totally confident of my abilities to create new direct business from the ground up, I walked in and told them to keep their "lists", keep their agencies, and that I was, in essence a new direct creating, account opening "machine" who would start from scratch. They ended up giving me a few grand per month in billing on the sports/talk station that I accepted since I would have been a fool not to do so. Let's examine, for a moment, my success with these three properties.

WDAB—the sports/talk station, had such a weak signal at the time and such a small audience that the average unit rate was around $30. Utilizing what I had learned in Albany from a genius in radio recruiting, Mr. Chris Stonick, who had visited the northeast and presented his radio recruitment program that he said he had developed to an exact science over 10-years, I went out and sought out human resource directors who were primarily looking for men 25-54 years old or for whom that was also a viable target demographic. I opened the Pepsi Cola Bottling Company by getting business from a local, recruitment budget. The job description said something about "being able to lift 50-pounds and to roll a dolly weighing over 100-pounds all day long." Not that a female couldn't perform those tasks but it was over 90% certain that they were looking for men 25-54. My startled co-workers kept asking: "You got Pepsi Cola?!!! How in the world did you ever do that?!!" My answer was the same as when I "got" Bank of America. I did it NOT by going to their MARKETING folks who would have referred me to a huge agency somewhere in New York city who would have laughed me off the phone or never returned a phone call, but rather to a totally different, completely local division with a completely separate budget, the local, area human resource recruiter who could make decision locally, and who usually just threw money aimlessly at a classified newspaper ad in the Sunday paper as most recruiters or HR departments did. After all, that was the established way of doing things.

I was even able to state to these people: "I actually HOPE you cancel before the end of your 4-week contract! Because that means that you'll have hired all of the people you need and that you'll definitely be back for the next hiring cycle." And that's exactly the way it worked. One time Pepsi called up and yelled over the phone: "Please!! Stop the insanity!" since they were buried up to their ears in applications and phone calls due to the 60-second radio recruitment ads. The Bank of America experience was even more unique.

Directly across from our radio stations main office sprang up a huge, city block-long building, outside of which waved a huge, but very simple banner that read just two words: "Now Hiring!" My car was in the shop and I had taken a ride to work that day. Looking across the street I stated "I think I'll go out and do some prospecting!" The gent who had driven me to work that day laughed and said: "You're not going out to do any prospecting today. Bob! Your car is in the shop, remember?!!! I answered very simply:

"I'm going out on foot." You could hear the roars of laughter from several sales staffs at once as they all screamed, hysterically: "You're going out on FOOT?!! Aaaaaaaaaha ha ha aaaaaaaaaa!" I walked across the street to this strange, non-descript building and in the door and up to the receptionist, and asked, sort of like a 'detective Colombo' clueless investigator:

"Excuse me, but I've just got to ask you…who in the hell are you, anyway? I just see a sign that says "NOW HIRING" but nothing about who you are." The girl answered:

"Oh, we're Bank of America." I guess it was a brand new, mammoth call center, just getting ready to open. When I asked why they didn't have a signage to that effect she whispered that it was a temporary drop-off location for dozens and dozens of armored cars, transporting over 50 million dollars in cash each day and thus they wanted to keep a low profile for about a month.

I was immediately ushered into the back room when a really nice lady named Ann Prosser, HR director, saw me without an appointment and about a week later 4 of our stations were broadcasting details of all of the various openings at the call center. I once again had to answer a bunch of "how in the hell did you?!!....." questions. The scenario was the same as with Pepsi Cola with a local budget. But the most significant thing about this success story was that the sales staffs of all 6 stations had to drive right past that building each morning, again twice while gong and coming from lunch, and then finally at the end of the day, and NOT ONE person thought to find out about the mysterious "Now Hiring!!" sign. I had done so, and had done so ON FOOT! I guess they call this the "Acres of Diamonds" principle which relates to a story about a farmer who traveled the entire world, seeking his fortune, only to return, unsuccessful, and then he looked out into his plowed fields to seem something gleaming in the sunlight. He discovered that his own fields, in his own backyard were littered with diamonds and he was therefore rich, with his 'fortune' right under his nose all the time!" The story is probably more of a parable, or a 'teaching moment' than having a basis in reality other than to illustrate a universal truth.

Also, at the time, since nobody was really bothering to sell such a small, low-rated radio station the management team tried to incentive the staff and raised the commission rate to 28%. Using radio recruiting and other principles that I had learned from the masters in the business within 6-months, coming from 1,300 miles out of town, by December of that year, 1999, I became the number one billing or producing salesman out of the 9 on our staff on this tiny sports talk station. I was writing between $20,000 and $25,000 per month and thus at 28% commission I was earning in excess of $6,000 per month off that little station and had two other properties to sell. One of my fellow reps, Sandra Hardy told me: "Oh, you're definitely our top biller on WDAB!!"

When I thought about that I considered that to be quite an accomplishment for just 6-months in the Tampa Bay region, especially starting with nearly nothing and not even knowing the basic geography or environs of where the hell I was!

My experiences in hitting my OTHER two budget goals, however, were definitely NOT to be so happy and 'go lucky'..............please read on....................................

CHAPTER SEVEN

INTO THE BELLY OF THE BEAST OF THE BIGGEST RADIO CONSOLODATORS AND MY "OTHER TWO" PROPERTIES TO SELL

I covered my astounding success with a little sports talk station in Chapter Six, but as I also mentioned, our sales staff wasn't exactly the envy of out 5 sister stations in the Carrier Wave Communications Tampa Bay cluster because we were also responsible for hitting our numbers with two other radio properties. We had WFLB, a great news/talk station and then we had the 'sports budget.' The later was part of the WFLB broadcasting but it was unique in many ways.

First of all I did fairly well with normal spot selling on WFLB and a few endorsement programs that were successful, but nothing like the teamwork I had achieved in Schenectady, New York with Mike O'Leary. Feeling strongly that I could duplicate my success with whomever was this station in Florida's 'afternoon guy" I quickly discovered that no advertiser wanted his services. I never met him but I heard his 'show' and it was just filled with hateful speech, negativity and non-stop put downs of his few callers. Radio recruitment, was, of course, somewhat successful but my ideas of "theme" show for medical groups run up against a brick wall. So much of what had worked well in one market simply didn't translate into this market. I tried my best, made hundreds of calls per week, but again and again, despite my 7-day per week efforts I ran into nothing but repeated rejection. I could say that this was during the 2,000 "dot.com bubble" meltdown of the stock market when potential advertisers were getting their first dose of a financial crisis in quite few years, following the budget surplus, booming stock market of the 90's. But I feel as I would be making excuses and so would anyone reading this.

I was only at Carrier Wave for about a year and a half and any person in sales will tell you that the natural cycle for sales is to have periodic peaks and valleys and that it's possible to have "a bad run." But since I was really "killing it" and making a ton of money at the sports talk station as outlined in the last chapter I didn't feel threatened and knew that, if given enough time, I would eventually, by maintaining an extremely high activity level, sell myself out of it. It was around this time that I also began to regret by bravado in telling the hiring manager to keep their lists and agencies. Newer salespeople who had been in the business we're coming in and being handed a substantial amount of billing business as they negotiated their positions at the station whereas I was totally 'slugging it out' from the trenches with nothing to start with. It was a struggle to say the least. Two main factors were in play, however, that caused me to leave this particular radio 'gig.' One was something that was literally impossible to sell without some seriously large accounts and another was an individual who you may have encountered as Satan, the devil, El Diablo, Adolph Hitler, or some other sheer human embodiment of evil incarnate, general sales manager, Chick Duncan! The two were totally intertwined in many ways.

Let's start with the first factor, our "sports budget." We were cajoled, threatened, pushed, cattle-prodded, and continuously brow beaten on a daily basis to sell on air sponsorships to this sports team, that, as previously mentioned, was at the very bottom of the league in its' win-loss record. They were the joke of the sport and just kept losing and losing and losing game after game. "Carrier Wave' however, thought they had a real "cash cow" on their hands, since they obviously paid millions and millions of dollars more than the broadcasting rights to this team's games were actually worth. It was a brand new team in the league and as experiences with say, the New York "Mets" baseball team when they started out in the early 1960's proved, a new team usually goes through this "laughing stock of the league" phase before they develop, start to gain a following, and start to fill up stadiums with paying fans, who will then increase revenue so that bigger name and more talented players can be brought in, etc. It's a process. Unfortunately for me and many other poor souls we were in a position of trying to sell sponsorships at extremely high unit rates to the early 1960's New York Mets! And I must state that I witnessed the totally unnecessary yet complete destruction of the careers of dozens and dozens of some of the most talented, trained, experienced, and previously, "Superstar status' sales people who were sacrificed on the altar of this "sports marketing" budget portion of our business. "Sports marketing" in itself is big business. But it's 'big business" in New York, Cincinnati, Atlanta, and other cities and regions where the teams have built huge and loyal fan bases, have immense budgets to hire the best talent, where the ballparks were either filled or near capacity and the revenue flowed relentlessly into the pockets of the owners from a multitude of sources. Plus these teams were generally playing way ahead of "500 ball" or winning more than losing. They were definitely at least, competitive!

Here was our 'deal.' WFLB was contracted to broadcast these, mostly night games that began around 7:30pm and generally ran until around 10:30pm. YOU, Mr. Advertiser, have a chance to become co-branded or a sponsor of these games. You'd be mentioned as a sponsor each time there was a pitching change, you were the "hit advertiser of the night" should all 9 players get a least one hit each, or you could buy mostly 15-second and 30-second radio commercials during the breaks in the game or when the innings were over and a new inning was to begin. The prices were staggering! A 15-second commercial went for around $350 and a 30-second went fetched $450. This would normally be utter insanity since these were technically "off prime-time"(Monday through Friday 6am-7pm is considered prime time for radio across the united States) commercials and this market sold prime time, 60-SECOND commercials for between $100 and $350 for, say, the top 10 highest rated radio stations. The audience being so much smaller after the 'evening drive time" period ended at 7pm and the radio audience evaporated to watch "TV time" that most radio station rates for "night time" commercials, 7pm to 12 midnight generally went for around $50, to reflect the value of the much tinier group of listeners. Some stations even gave away later evening commercials to maintain their top-of-the-rate card "prime time" rates or to massage the schedule, perhaps to get on an agency 'buy."

How in the hell could we justify $350 and $450 rates for night time audiences. Well look no further, Mr. Advertiser! Did you realize that your message will not only air in the immediate Tampa Bay market, but it will SIMULTANEOUSLY air on 15 other radio stations that were simulcasting the games?!! Your message will be heard 250 miles away in Jacksonville Florida! Also 100 miles away in Orlando! 150 miles away in Daytona Beach! Heck, your business will be known throughout most of the state!! You'll get 16 stations for those $350 and $450 evening rates!!

Do I really have to tell you what happened? It you have any rationality as I'm sure you do you can almost guess at the response.

"I own two car dealerships here in Saint Petersburg. I already know from my own research that 90% of my customers come from a 15 miles radius around my dealerships. I don't care HOW many stations are hearing my message! Nobody is going to drive 100, 150, or 250 miles from Jacksonville to visit my showrooms. They'd have to drive past at least 20 of my closer competitors selling the exact same vehicle lines as I am to get here!! That just doesn't happen!! And I can buy evening spots on most local radio stations for 20 bucks for a 60-second spot! $350?! $450?? For 15-seconds?!! Are you nuts?!!" or,

"Those are biggest losers in the entire league!! I don't want to associate my business with those bums! They can't even sell more than 8,000 seats out of a 40,000-seat stadium! Are you nuts?!!"

Even "Jimmy Hawkins" who was, at the time, the "sports budget" manager, admitted: "It's an EMOTIONAL sell. You'd NEVER be able to rationalize that kind of cash outlay unless you were selling 'the sizzle.'" It wouldn't make any sense for simply the numbers, he admitted. You'd never be able to justify it as a viable return on investment! Then if follows that it wouldn't make any sense to any business person either! Oh, there were a handful of enterprises that indeed DID have an interest in reaching the whole state. Florida Power, was a statewide enterprise. The Florida Ford dealer's Association was another. But unless you were able to get to the president of Pizza Hut, or the president of Avis rent-A-Car, or some other completely walled off, unapproachable entity you didn't even have a ghost of a chance of even making a presentation. And yet we were constantly hounded, threatened, and cattle-prodded to make such a sale! Eventually, I made a bunch of appointments, invited the "big boys" out to "close them" sine I must be doing something wrong in my execution, only to find out that these "hot shots" COULD NOT close the sale either! What is wrong, guys?!!

That brings me to the totally intertwined, aforementioned, "human" part of this impossible equation. Let's talk for a moment about Mr. Chick Duncan. This was another one of "the consolidators" hand-picked puppets. He couldn't sell his way out of a ripped piece of plastic wrap but somehow, through some 'connection' somewhere, he sat in a big office as general sales manager to all 6 stations in the cluster. He was a hateful monster of a human being and I describe him in this way since I don't want to start using obscene or off color language since that's just a sign of a limited vocabulary. But I WILL tell you this. He had a picture of Adolph Hitler on his desk, his "hero", a symbol of hate, evil, destruction and human suffering. Chick was a soulless, gutless, ravaging 'thing' that could not be described as human. He firmly believed in "motivating' by bashing, insulting, threatening, talking-down to and otherwise negatively badgering his sales force, actually thinking that that kind of behavior would someone make them 'straighten up and fly right' when in reality all it did was to cause people to completely DESPISE their jobs, or even coming to work.

We were met each morning by hateful, threatening e-mails on our computers to start our day, frequent visits to our cubicles as he got in the faces of the sales people and demanded why they weren't selling more, and vitriolic speeches in sales meetings that were full of nothing but negativity, complaints, and personal put downs. It was so savage that right before the beginning of the sports season selling processes the brightest and best sales professionals who had been there and had been put through this gauntlet the previous year were quitting ahead of the coming 'storm from hell.' I'll be either quoting if not outright reproducing a few of one of my mentors, advisors, and experts in this kind of subhuman treatment on a national scale's daily blogs; Mr. Jerry Del Colliano, who has done battle with one of the big consolidators and whose credentials include:

- Advisor to New Media & Broadcasting
- Consultant to Higher education
- Clinical Professor Music Industry
- University of Southern California (04-08)

My perspective is limited to sub-human animals like this piece of trash, Chick Duncan. But Jerry has a national perspective and has seen this exact kind of "management" behavior happen all throughout the world of consolidation, and from every corner of the country.

The bright side to this advisor is that you'll not only hear some unbelievable 'war stories' such as this last one as well as the ones that were revealed in Chapter One of this book, or the one that the above Hitler protégé' so vehemently executed on dozens and dozens of the cream of the crop of radio sales people, but you'll see a great number of positive suggestions as to how this whole sick situation could have been prevented. You'll be introduced to some folks who are not taking this brutal "low road" to please the stockholders, bankers, and finance people in Ivory towers. You'll see that it didn't have to be like this and that there ARE some valid, creative, and effective solutions to it all.

But again I digress. Let me finish up with this monster, masquerading as a human being, Mr. Chick

Duncan, who certainly has, with untold others like him, a secure reservation in the hottest part of hell. Or, if he's really lucky, he'll "get his" right here on this earth!

To finish with Mr. Duncan. First he blew through 20 or 30 of radio's finest talents; folks who took off to local competitors, all the way to Colorado, or who were so "damaged" the way one female rep phrased it, that they left the business they had once loved altogether, never to return---which in itself is a tragedy beyond proportion to its description. He ended up being bounced out to door himself eventually and was using his connections to assume another similar position, hundreds of miles away, where I'm sure he's spreading misery around another group of people, or , if the world is at all lucky, he's lying down stone cold dead and on his assigned route to the depths of hell.

Let me leave you with this. As I saw him going down the line of cubicles, firing one person after another, having cut our commissions in half as punishment and not making the position even viable financially, I jumped ship and went to work for short while at a sports manufacturing business. But that's story of another psycho and another book. Let's finish this chapter up with "Chick."

The Internet had developed by 2000 into an intricate tool and the company introduced a program where one sales person had the ability to create a nationwide Internet program that could be duplicated in all 1,200 stations for the right advertiser. I and a friend from one of our sister stations found one. Well, I found him but my partner helped me develop this program. It was with a gentleman who had just sold his business, was in the new business of

"CMA" or continuing medical education and who had hundreds of contacts, from the business he had just sold, with every major pharmaceutical company in the United States. His desire was to 'take this thing national!' This "thing" was a program of continuing web casts or 'webinars' that would be accessed on demand by doctors, specialists, and every medial field to keep up with the rapidly expanding knowledge base of the medical industry, and to maintain their various certifications. We would promote these seminars on most of our stations and implement the on-demand" webinars" in conjunction with the radio introductions. Many managers were telling us that just ONE such program would immediately produce a 'six-figure paycheck" for the creative sales person, who would be compensated for his local billing plus an override for the national component.

We worked closely with a gal named "Donna' I'll call her, out of Orlando, where these programs were developed, and after several months of such effort, produced a CD disc with a proposal on it, along with a full PowerPoint description of all of the moving parts.

Trouble was, neither my buddy, Phil nor I could open the attachment on the screens of our computers---- remember this was the year 2000.

Unbeknownst to us, "Chick" had been talking with Donna at a sales manager's conference in Orlando and asked her: "How does this all work, Donna? How does a local person put together a national program and get paid for all 1,200 stations?! I don't get it?" She laughed hysterically right into Chick's face as and answered: "Well your SALESPEOPLE certainly get it, Chick!! Go ask David Lear, he's got a 20 MILLION DOLLAR national proposal sitting on his desk right now!!" Now remember, David Lear himself didn't even know what he had sitting on his desk. After all he didn't have the ability on his computer to even OPEN the god-blasted thing! We finally found a guru of technology who was able to help us open up the disc and we immediately printed it out. As is wont to happen the very last page came flying out of the computer from the top of the stack of papers and drifted slowly to the floor. Phil and I immediately began howling with laughter as we saw the last column that said:

"TOTAL INVESTMENT: 20 MILLION DOLLARS." But if the majority of the nation's pharmaceutical companies were going to jointly fund it, and it was a NATIONAL program, the numbers really weren't' that off the scale. They certainly WERE to us since this would certainly dwarf by a factor of several hundred at least, the largest sale that any radio group had ever made! As we laughed , Mr. Chick Duncan, was driving back to Tampa, tightly gripping his steering wheel and gritting his teeth in rage, having just been 'dressed down' by corporate.

He ushered Phil and I into his office, slammed the door, behind us, and said: "When were you guys going to tell me about this?!!!! We answered with the absolute truth:

"Chick!" we pleaded, "We didn't even know what "THIS" was going to be until 15-minutes ago when we finally discovered what they were proposing!!" "We didn't know what was in it!!" Completely ignoring the significance of what was lined up to be the largest pending sale of any one radio station in the entire United States of America. "Chip" spoke to us in a seething, snake-like tone:

"You guys made me look like a fool!!!" We attempted t interrupt but he kept on going:

"And when you make me look like a fool....... it really pisses me off!!!"

Such was the insanity of one of the big, hot shot 'consolidators.' I left the company two weeks later and since I had established the relationship with the customer and Phil barely knew him, the whole project lost momentum, gradually unraveled without my personal attention, and then completely fell apart, drifting away in the summer breeze, like a feather shorn from the body of a buckshot-filled falling bird. Welcome once again to the now dying world, or radio consolidator and just one instance of one of the sleazy, slimy snakes, who helped bring it all crashing down around them. Please read a recent blog or two of Jerry's to see if you can pick out the real name of 'Carrier Wave Communications" or where it finally as of late 2009, eventually led........................

CHAPTER EIGHT

"THE WDCT YEARS'

You'll hear more about innovation and ways that the current radio model can be salvaged. Thanks to Jerry Del Colliano, and with his permission and through and his insights we've seen a few great ideas. The whole crisis seems to involve what is called "Radio's Lost Generation", the 80 million plus "Generation Y" audience, who now have so many choices in how to interact with media, music, and information that they no longer need radio the way previous generations did. These young folks may be currently 12 to 24 years old now. But before you know it they'll be in that 'sweet spot' of buying power, the" Holy Grail" of "25-54" or the age group that most advertisers think spend the most money. The radio industry is starting to lose this huge generation, bigger even the 'baby boomers" that have been called the "pig in the python' since their habits, lifestyle and behavior has always dominated the entire nation's development as they moved through various life cycles. As an added slap in the face to the industry, the 'boomers' as well as the 65+ crowd are also embracing the various new social media and technological alternatives to radio listening. It's a complete social tsunami!!

But back to the timeline where we left off. After leaving "Carrier Wave" in late 2000 as they continued to throw the brightest and best overboard or cause them to be so 'damaged' that they no longer wished to work under such horrendous conditions, I "stepped out' of the business myself and went to work for a sports manufacturer. Since this has nothing to do with radio except for my being amongst the waves of people of people leaving it, let it suffice to say that it involved yet another psycho at the helm, and ended after about 6-months with a worker's compensation claim. This was caused my an injury I sustained in my back as the president, vice-president, C.E.O, sales manager and a little gentleman from Peru all stood over me, yelling like a group of cheerleaders: "Yeah gotta lift!!! Yeah gotta lift!!!" What they were yelling for me to lift was a 1,500 crate of show materials that had been unprofessionally tacked together and was falling apart after a recent trade show. I'm not saying that I'm a "little guy" but I WAS 51-years old at the time and what I HAD to lift weighed 1,500 pounds. I yanked out my back and went on worker's compensation for a few months as I underwent therapy from several doctors.

With the glowing recommendation from dozens of former managers and co-workers, as well as extremely overjoyed former clients (Check out "Testimonials" on my personal marketing website, www.bob-curran-consultant.com.) I was introduced to another radio consolidator group, "DCT Communications" in January of 2001. Everybody was telling me to "Go see Mike" and then rattled off his last name without me phonetically being able to recognize it or spell it accurately. I had contacted him while still on worker's compensation since my injury was improving gradually and we talked several times on the phone. He obviously had interacted with my first employer, "Great Dane Media" since he yelled over the phone, in a completely joking manner: "I'd never hire anybody who worked for Great Dane!! They were the biggest bunch of losers in the industry!!"

"Mike" was one of the "GSM's" or general sales managers of one of the 5-station cluster at "DCT" in Tampa Bay. They basically played an "oldies" format which concentrated on "the greatest hits of the 60's and 70's." Although a music format was not my first choice, they had decent ratings and were profiled by some of their former employers as a much better work environment than the inferno of hell that was "Carrier Wave Communications" and there was no sports budget to sell, with $450, 30-second, commercials at night.

When I first met with "Mike" he looked vaguely familiar, and he did a kind of "double take" when we first met as well, as if he knew me from someplace. The radio business is so fluid, with so many sales people moving from station to station, most of them in search of just the perfect "list" so they have a guaranteed income, that anything is possible. Once again I made the error of walking in and telling him to keep his "list' keep his agencies, and that I was there as a "new direct account opener." He introduced me to every single layer of management in the building, all of whom were impressed with my interviewing skills, my work history and my resume' and then I was offered the paltry sum of a $2,000 per month guarantee. I thought it to be kind of insulting, given my experience, but had to admit to myself that since I was 'selling myself' as a self-generating income producing entity that I would eventually be writing my own ticket or paycheck anyway. These sales positions are ultimately commission-based pay models anyway. So I accepted the offer.

What I didn't know was that about a year before I came on board, your 'guarantee', no matter what the amount, generally lasted for 12 months. The normal "sales cycle" can easily run 90-days or more from first contact until "closing" of a campaign. Recently it had been shortened to 6-months before you were totally on your own, paid only on commission. Right before I joined the organization a whole new system was instituted, that one sales person who came on board right after I did called the program, succinctly. The "90 days and your out!" program. In other words, I had 3 months at $2,000 per month and then I was completely thrown to the wolves on a commission only basis. And since I was starting with zip, zero, and zilch as my "list" I indeed had quite the uphill "challenge" in front of me. If I can skip ahead let me tell you that I was there for a full three years until January 2004 before I was hired away by an even better, much more lucrative offer from competitor that I simply couldn't refuse ($5,000 per month guarantee for a full 6 months) but the point is that I 'made it' as the first 'poster child' for the "90-days and you're out" program, whereas the other sales person who had coined that particular expression did not.

It was during these three years 2,001-2,004 that I truly "cranked it up." I began opening accounts left and right, once establishing a record that most folks feel will NEVER be equaled let alone exceeded, opening 22 new direct accounts over a period of 23 weeks—not one of them ever having done radio before!

But let's back up just a little bit. Right after I was hired something stuck in my mind. WHERE did I know this "Mike" guy from?? Did he used to work at Carrier Wave? Did I know him from some social networking group? Did we have some mutual friends where we had interacted before? THEN it hit me!! This was none other than 'Rughead' Mike Remeedy!! The snake from 1.200 miles north of Tampa Bay! The lowlife I had run into, although not at my particular station, during my brief 6-month, "living an invitational lie" period in northeast Pennsylvania in 1996!! This was the piece of human slime that "motivated" his sales team by threatening them each day with "DON'T COME BACK WITHOUT AN ORDER!!" I hadn't known him well since we barely saw each other during that dark time, except for the fact that he had shown his true colors and went out and snaked account from me to his station from mine by employing negative and totally unrepresentative selling techniques. Well, I had come this far, I thought. I might as well make a 'go' of it anyway. At least we were both now on the same 'team' and he had no motivation to bad mouth my station since it was also his. A few things sat as roadblocks in my way however, that were both major and previously unheard of in this business.

The main one was that a great part of Mike's compensation came from the fact that he was set up to carry and be partially paid for maintaining his own "list." We had a system that handled the 'call-ins' of people looking to possibly advertise on our "oldies' station, all of which were directed through the manager, in this case 'ole "Rughead" himself. Now who do you suppose ended up with the pick of the litter or the cream of the crop of these call-ins?!! The sales force as was the norm on our 4 other 'sister stations?" Or a certain gentleman who looked like he was wearing a helmet? The arrangement was akin to making the sales manager compete against his own sales staff for new business. Insane? Once again I want to keep it clean or I'd use other language! He gave himself away many Monday mornings as he came in with the bottom part of the back of his hair glowing a bright green from the chlorine in his swimming pool. His wig was just one of the things about him that was phony. It was the outward manifestation of a malignancy of character than ran deep and throughout his entire set of behavior; his entire being. Luckily and fairly for the sales staff, upper management changed this 'twilight zone" arrangement after my first year or so there and we were on a level playing field with the other stations as to the equitable distribution of leads. His lack of any type of moral compass was, however, to be a theme that ran through the entirety of the operation during my three year tenure at DCT Communications.

I not only survived the "90 days and you're out" nearly impossible program but prospered once again due to my love of new business development, continuously going into the unknown to "sell myself, sell my company", etc. I seemed to be able to 'score' someone's trust during that first 45-seconds when people immediately 'size you up' and either trust you or don't. This phenomenon is ancient. It goes back to the days of 'flight or fight' that is hard-wired into our brains. Ancient humans had to immediately decide if a new encounter was friend or foe for their own survival. Today we still have that almost instant 'first impression' that is largely unconscious in nature and that is most likely not only innate, but is further refined throughout our life as we meet various people of all, uh, 'stripes' in our daily human interactions. My 'act' was in fact no 'act' at all in that I was 100% naturally David Lear, with all of my strengths as well as imperfections. I never tried to be a second-rate Dale Carnegie or Wayne Dyer but absolutely genuinely myself. And that seemed to come through to the prospect immediately. This ability to instantly disarm one's suspicions and fears is something that I guess you're born with, but can also be developed or honed to near perfection over time. It's the old 'nurture versus nature' argument from my college psychology classes. It's a discussion that can go on and on forever as to which is more important, but never fully answered.

A very sales savvy gentleman, Mike Anderson, I believe his name is, who heads a media consulting group called the Center For Sales Strategy, or CSS, recently wrote a book, the title of which, at the moment, escapes me, but which made a great deal of sense. The subject involved the normal process of how a new media account is developed. The logic is totally clear to me based on my experience and directly relates to the subject of relationship-building alluded to in the last paragraph. What normally happens is an "AE" or account executive or account manager, or as some insulting fools put it, "the seller" (that's like calling a Mercedes a 'transporter') prospects for new business that they feel is appropriate for their particular media property. The prospective client is an advertiser, they're sufficiently large enough, they obviously spend a great deal of advertising dollars somewhere, and they definitely have a need to get the word out to differentiate them from the competition and/or to educate the general public as to what they do. They also fit well with the particular media property's audience profile. So the rep makes his or her 100 phone calls, e-mails, seed letters, mailings, etc. They get 3 or 4 solid appointments and then they meet for the first time with the prospect.

What happens next is of vital importance. According to Mike Anderson, as well as my own experiences in the business, the media rep then does some sort of interview or customer needs analysis to uncover what the key marketing challenges of the prospective client seem to be. Then, armed with this knowledge the rep returns to their station and assembles the most beautiful proposal they can, with all kinds of charts and graphs, laid out beautifully; often using the customer's own words and expressions to play back to them in the body of the proposal. If the "seller" is really lucky, they get a second appointment to present the proposal. They then "present" their proposal, utilizing every single strategy they've been taught, logically and dramatically attempting to get the prospect's signature on something. Oftentimes the customer wants to 'think about it' or 'run it by' someone else to get the final "o.k." The salesperson often leaves with half-baked, very positive assurances from the prospect and the words 'looks good' or "I like it but let me run it by my wife…she's the boss." Herein lays the fatal flaw or several fatal flaws.

First of all the prospect hasn't really had the chance to get to know the salesperson enough to trust them completely. After all they've been "had" before by a car dealer, an insurance agent, a clown behind the counter of a retail establishment, a telemarketer, or anyone else to 'close a quick sale.' Second, if the 'wife' is indeed part of the decision making process, if not the final decision-maker, where they hell was she when this process was going down?! The salesperson has awkwardly put the prospect into the role of being the "media expert' with the task of having to do the media person's job and to have to "sell" it to someone else. This is a sure 'sales death' experience. All the "wife' or the "big boss" upstairs has to do is to come up with one objection or reason not to proceed and the person who was presented this great big, ornate "proposal' folds in fear of the unknown or fear of making the wrong decision.

What usually and tragically transpires after that is that the salesperson continually 'follows up' with phone call after phone call, e-mail after e-mail, continuously hounding and pounding on the prospect, since, in the salesperson's mind, it's all but a done deal! One of my managers in the wholesale food business in L.A. once described that particular farce by saying: "When you do that, Bob, you let the customer make a monkey out of you!! And no customer is going to make a monkey out of me!!" In the meantime, the proud sales rep goes back and tells his boss that he's 90% sure (or is 67.3%?--here we go again) that it's 'going to close.' The poor sap then becomes what we have called a 'radio stalker!'

Mike Anderson said to slow down. Have not just that first meeting but arrange another meeting, this one with the wife or the 'big boss man' or the receptionist for that matter!! Make sure that it's not just one person trying to "sell" another person on something. Make it a true partnership. Get on THEIR said of the desk, strategize over the course of successive meetings, and explore different approaches as if you were working for the client's company in their advertising department. But by all means avoid the "maybes" at all cost or you'll be riding a merry-go-round of "maybes"" right into the streets, your valuable time here on earth literally robbed from you by virtue of your own behavior.

Another great sales coach, Mr. Greg Bennett, president of Bennett Productivity Programs Inc. urges you to "take them to a no." That's right, "take them to a NO." It's human nature for the prospective buyer to not want to hurt the feelings of the seller by letting them down. They also don't want to create a situation where they cause the seller to 'ramp up' his efforts and start pounding them with numbers and logic and pressuring them into making a decision they may subsequently regret. So they take the middle ground and say things like "let me think about it", "looks good" "I'm fairly sure I'll get approval from…." And the merry-go-round ride starts…right to failure! And yet this is the way that the majority of sales situations begin and proceed to absolutely nowhere... It has been going on like this a surely as the revolving door has been spinning reps out the door. Greg Bennett's take is that you'll eventually close a few "no's" since they might just be indications that you haven't answered all of their questions, concerns, or objections, and further meetings need to take place. But you'll never, ever close a "maybe!" He even teaches specific things to say, like: "Well, let's agree that you're saying 'no…for now.'" Unless you establish that true and lasting "partnership" with your target account you might make a sale or two. But you'll be so far off the mark that they probably won't renew or cancel before the end of the contract since you didn't fully establish their realistic expectations up front in your rush to "close a quick sale' for fear of what that mean old boss will greet you with when you return empty handed at the end of the day. And situations like this are directly attributable to this 'don't come back without a sale' mentality or endless sales meetings where you learn the 'tricks' on how to get someone to sign something. Nobody likes to be manipulated, nobody wants to be tricked. But everyone wants a true ally; everyone wants a reliable consultant, a 'business partner' with a true vested interest in their business.

I was fortunate enough to meet one of the most talented sales people I've ever had the pleasure of working with when I was at "DCT" a Mr. Tom Frankly. He joked and laughed with and so entertained his customers over the phone that they really got to know him intimately as person over time. And this approach so endeared him to his clients, often agencies hundreds of miles away whom he never even met face-to-face, that he developed that important trusting relationship and did a tremendous amount of business at "DCT." He still had to put up with the top-down, continuous pressure from each level of management, answering to higher above, continuously cattle-prodding for results from below, but I have to hand it to Tom. He refused to play that stupid game.

Once, as he stood beside his immediate boss at two urinals in a men's room, the boss, asked Tom, for probably the 20th time that week:

"So, Tom…. Have you got any closers today?" Tom shot back:

"You ask me that one more time and I'm going to pee on your shoes!!" That's the type of 'real person' sales professional I am as well. And it immediately 'comes through' to the customer. And yet these consolidators again and again take their eyes off the ball, and running scared like tiny mice, continue to throw bodies against the fray! Let's cut the customer a break here. After you've received the 25th call of the day, with nearly the identical salutation, which is usually:

"CAN I SPEAK TO THE PERSON WHO HANDLES YOUR ADVERTISING, PLEASE?" (I know the proper English usage is "May I…?") Usually delivered by 'the new guy' in the same droning monotone voice, you're probably ready to simply tell what they call 'the gatekeeper' usually the receptionist, something like, "our advertising is already spent for the next 200 years!" or something designed to blow off the poor sap who is just trying to make a living.

Thus again I at least partially blame the "consolidators" who continuously hire and fire drones like this, continuously throw new flesh against an impenetrable wall, and force legitimate sales professionals to have to constantly walk in the footsteps of these people who shouldn't be on the phone 'soliciting' like this to begin with!! But why not just blame the salespeople?? They must not be 'working' hard enough!! Get out that threat! Get out that cattle-prod!! Don't they think that these so carefully-screened people they originally hired WANT to make the sale? Don't they realize that these people have bills to pay and families to feed?!!

BACK TO THE CHRONOLOGIAL ORDER OF MY CAREER AT "DCT"

Armed with no "list" no "agency buys' regularly coming in, which is basically order taking not sales, by my second year I had developed what turned out to be the SECOND-HIGHEST BILLING ACCOUNT ON THE OLDIES STATION out of the top 20. It was also the only 'direct' account on this list, as opposed to agencies, and it took a major supermarket chain to beat me out of the number one slot. The story of how it came about is worth telling.

Using what I'll call the "Mike Anderson/Greg Bennett" model, I approached a plastic surgery practice in Trinity, Florida, and after a good 45-minute trip one way. I met with the doctor, his wife who was his marketing director, again with the doctor, again with his wife, and worked diligently with them both together, becoming a trusted partner. Once we had developed and redeveloped and idea together it was simply a matter of driving the 45 minute to an hour ride and picking up a check. Well low and behold, even confirming a solid appointment the 'wife' decided that my time, my efforts, and a chunk of my time here on this earth wasn't even worth canceling the confirmed appointment and simply didn't show up. I left, totally disgusted and insulted after putting in so much time and effort and on my way back I happened to see a scrolling electric sign that said "World Wellness Institute and Anti-Aging Center." It seemed a bit hokey but I was lucky to catch the advertising director available, and, after several more appointments and 'demo' tapes (we called them 'spec' commercials) I was able to create an ongoing advertising program that lasted for two years. They were investing some where north of $100,000 per year on my "oldies' station and another $30,000 per year on one of our 'sister' stations that was basically a Jazz format since the doctor loved Jazz music. At an 18% or 20% commission rate they were my biggest account the SECOND largest billing account of the entire station. I guess I had turned lemons into lemonade as I returned from my time-wasting failure with the plastic surgeon!

"Rughead" Mike Remeedy had to be aware of this success and was usually full of compliments:

"I'd put you up against ANYONE I've ever known in this business!" he once said. Another time, in front of an agency, Mike gushed: "David calls on accounts that no other radio rep would even ever think of calling on!!" I developed such a great relationship with the anti-aging account that whenever a competing radio station would hear their ads and call on the advertising manager he'd tell them: "You'll have to run it by my advertising director, David Lear, at the oldies station first." Naturally my phone never rang in this regard.

It certainly wasn't all a bed of roses at "DCT" however. We had an animal with a short fuse who oversaw all of the commercial production. Let's call him Joel Burns, although most sales folks had some, shall we say, "More intensely descriptive names" for him. He, with the clueless, passive backing of upper management rode roughshod over the sales force. He was rude, insulting and nearly impossible to work with without some type of yelling confrontation. When this had happened at my first radio job back in Schenectady I had once responded to an insulting barrage from "little Mike' the studio gopher by leaving him a return message that "people have to sop beating the shit out of each other here!!" The 'legendary' morning man who had been there 20-years said that he had heard about the exchange. My first response was to begin to say that: '…yeah I guess I overreacted…." but Don Day jumped right in to say:

"No! You're absolutely right! I totally agree with you!! Goddamn it!! We're all in this together, and if we can't get along what the hell kind of organization have we got?!!" Thank you Don. The perspective is right on as well as appreciated.

What some of these clowns didn't realize and refused to" get", was that we were in the COMMUNICATION business! Our commercial messages were, in fact, our ultimate PRODUCT! And our ultimate 'mission' according to every one of them right up the ladder was to go out and get new direct business then we first had to demonstrate exactly what our message was, how it was to be delivered, complete with emphasis and vocal inflections, background music---the works!! "Joel's' take was that we should have complete 100% customer approval of the script itself, that 'demo' or 'spec' commercials were just wasting his time, and that the prospect, even one who had never done any radio before, should be able to tell from just a few paragraphs on a piece of paper whether to sign a contract or not. That wasn't anywhere near reality in the world of new direct business and it never will be!! I want to sell you a pair of shoes and I've told you that I have your size, size 11, now sign right here!! About two years into my 3 year 'run' "Joel" was finally bounced into the parking lot but only after a ton of salespeople's complaints and hundreds of thousands of dollars in lost sales and lost salespeople.

I kept hoping that my efforts, expertise, and record-breaking performances would earn me my share of call-ins or new business being thrown at least a little bit my way. But somehow they all rationalized, from the vice-president on down, that, as the V.P. once put it when I asked for my share of the new call-ins: "But you're so good at going out after direct business that we'd be taking valuable time away from your efforts by feeding you agencies and new call-ins." Lesser talented individuals thus were 'kept afloat' by being handed never-ending business while I struggled from the bottom up all the way.

The final straw was when an account that I had developed and serviced over a three-year period was unfairly taken from me and given to our "national' sales rep who was nothing more than an order-taker that I decided that I'd look elsewhere. I had several interview with various other radio groups and one day, one of them, whose offer I had refused as not being worth my "jumping ship" for came calling with the $5,000 per month guarantee as well as an offer of a substantial "list." After my experience at DCT and previous experiences, I had promised myself that making great strides as new account development specialist, starting with absolutely nothing, would be a mistake I would never repeat again. So I accepted the offer at Crux communications and remained there for over 5 years, becoming fully vested in their pension program that I will begin to receive when I turn 65 and an offer to return anytime I'd like. Finally I had found a corporate culture I could live with and it was to be the best "'run" of my radio career.

"JIMMY-JOE MEEKER" TO THE RESCUE

This business can be extremely nerve-wracking, producing constant worry of being fired since you're "only as good as your last sale" an have to prove yourself again and again every day. So at DCT someone once gave me a shrill, loud whistle and I created a 'character' called "Jimmy-Joe Meeker." Mr. Meeker was a character I played over the phone when we ran into a 100% hopeless cause who had wasted a salesperson's time or was unusually rude and obnoxious, even beyond the normal abuse we had to take each day. As a fellow rep named "Sara" once put it:

"The way they treat us!!!" Don't they think that radio reps are potential customers too?!!" Well old Jimmy-Joe knew what to do. The name "Jimmy-Joe-Meeker" came from a fake character name that Jim Rockford, James Garner, used to employ in the series "The Rockford Files" when he was pulling a scam on someone. As a last resort, and only employed against the lowest of the low, when there was absolutely no chance at getting an appointment or making a sale. "Jimmy-Joe" would usually call the prospect or sometimes the rude 'gatekeeper' and alternately blow his whistle into the phone and yell: "Hi, thar!! This is Jimmy-Joe Meeker callin'. "Hear THAT, darlin'? (Double whistle blow.) THAT'S the train of opportunity. It's pullin' out of the station and YOU ain't on it!!! JIMMY-JOE-MEEK-ER!!! I'm JIMMY-JOE MEEK-ER!!(Double whistle blow). JIMMY-JOE MEEK-ER!!!!" The phone would then be pounded down on the desk in between a few more toots of the whistle and then the receiver would be slammed down, ending in the insane call. Dozens of sales people used to gather around my desk as I did this, vicariously living and relieving their daily stress through the crazy actions of "'ole Jimmy-Joe." Unprofessional? You bet! A great and necessary stress-reliever? Absolutely. Even management often answered the report of an especially rude prospect with the instructions to: "Ohhhh...Have Bob Jimmy-Joe Meeker 'em!!"(Just a side bar and a little humorous footnote to break up the sadness of some of this chapter.)

But again I jump ahead of myself. There is a letter, from a number of completely demoralized sales people at "DCT" that if I can edit, will tell you what became of them as they descended into complete anarchy and debauchery. It precipitated an ongoing, major lawsuit from several sales people so I'll have to be careful. But I CAN tell you that while I was there I saw instances of physically writing commercials onto the published commercial logs, double-billing clients for the same schedule, and other illegalities that eventually resulted in investigations from both the F.B.I. as well as the Federal Communications Commission that would definitely endanger the station's license as well as put a number of individuals in jail for a long time.

Two of the general sales managers as well as most upper management and even the market manager or market vice-president were to be summarily bounced down two flights of stairs, relocated to the far corners of the earth, and the first one to be banished was our old friend, "Rughead Remeedy' who had his dirty, unethical, illegal hands all over the whole situation. I was happy to have left in 2004. I finally returned to a non-consolidator, family-owned and run business

I'll leave you with THIS little gem about "DCT" that will pale in relation to the letter to corporate and the resulting suit. "9-11-2001" was definitely a shattering moment for our entire country. It was supposedly a time we "all came together as Americans!" Not so with the radio consolidators. "DCT" used it as an excuse to really 'clean house", summarily firing the HR director, a business manager, an accounts receivable gal, on air personalities, and many other decent worthwhile folks. I made the sarcastic comment at the time about the situation when I said: "It's good to see that we're all coming together as Americans over this!!"

In a subsequent mass-annihilation, right after the housing bubble crash, and stock market bubble meltdown, one of the best on air entertainers was bounced out in the "bloodbath." I'll call this individual "Magical Mark." "Magical" once told me: "Bob, you've done more for me and my wife than any other salesman I've ever worked with! Indeed I did. Through the power of trading endorsement fees for services I was able to:

1. Refinance his mortgage at a greatly reduced rate and allow him to pull out some badly-need cash.
2. Equip his entire home with new flooring.
3. Arrange for his wife to have a series of free dermatological treatments.

He'll always be a great personal and professional reference as well as yet another example of my production and the quality of my work. But speaking of the dot. com bubble burst, "9-11' and the consequent blow to the economy, the housing and wall street meltdown, the complete erasing of 40% of the world's worth, as well as our destroyed savings and 401-K's, our retirement dreams crushed---I have found the culprit!! It's the radio sales people! THEY'RE responsible for all of this!! They caused all of this!! Or at least you would tend to think so by the way they're expected to produce and succeed by the consolidators. The same consolidators who took a once thriving business and completely drove it into the ground with debt loads they can't service, banks taking them over, moral so completely destroyed that everyone's completely miserable all of the time. Thanks, guys! You're one great big group representing the "captains of industry!!"

Luckily there ARE solutions out there!! Let's take a look at a few of them with the help of my mentor, Jerry........

CHAPTER NINE

THE GOOD, THE BAD, THE UGLY, "WAR STORIES' RECENT AND CURRENT DEVELOPMENTS AND SOME SOLID SOLUTIONS AND POWERFUL SUGGESTIONS ON HOW RADIO CAN BE REVIVED AND IMPROVED IN LIGHT OF TODAY'S TECHNOLOGICAL AND SOCIEOLOGICAL ADVANCES AND DEVELOPMENTS

I know, that's quite a mouthful. But I'll try to "wind down" what will probably have to be "VOLUME ONE" of "DEAD AIR" on some positive and powerfully creative notes and suggestions on how the radio business can be both salvaged and improved. It's always advisable to have a positive attitude. We all know that. And yet, let's face it. It's indeed difficult if not impossible to describe what a negative pattern of behavior is inherently without talking about some of the seamier actions of some less than reasonable or outright inane business decisions that have been made in the industry.

So we'll be looking both backward and forward in the next few chapters. So far the content has been mostly about my personal journey through the industry since 1994 with the 'role playing on both Christmas and New Year's Eves' So stopping for a moment 10 years into my 15-year journey seems appropriate at this time for some reflection and some input from some of 'the masters" of this business. Moving forward let me just reiterate that I reentered the realm of family-owned and operated radio business in January 2004 and did remarkably well. 5 years, of again leading the field in new direct account development, called the "poster child" for the way the company envisioned new account openings to proceed, according to the vice president, and fully vested in the pension program with a huge certificate of appreciation from the CEO and company president. I did not get a 'gold watch" but received a nice little digital camera.

Again no business model is perfect and 4 commission cuts over 5 years certainly hurts as does the installation of a new technological nightmare of a computer system that robbed an entire cluster of their selling time, resulting in approximately 65% of the brightest and best to leave a company and often the entire business. This is one important point I'd like to make at this juncture.

I took the Dale Carnegie Public Speaking and Human relations course in 1980 and went on to use these principles to carve out an astonishingly successful sales career in several different businesses. I read all of the books, and then, when in L.A. in the food service business, had the chance to take the follow up course, The Dale Carnegie Sales Course. We learned a great deal. But the salient point I took from this 13-week marathon was the value of actual SELLING TIME. It seems a bit obvious but what they hammered into our heads over this 13-week period was that our most valuable resource was our SELLING TIME. After all, the whole of what we did was SALES and thus anything, anywhere, anytime that took time away from our SELLING TIME was directly detrimental and completely destructive to what was the essence of what we were hired to do!

If it seems like I'm belaboring the obvious but it's really not so, in that so many of these radio groups have essentially turned their sales people into some sort of "clerks." I'm talking about filling out endless reports, creating 'projections' struggling and fighting with computers crashing and technology throwing up roadblocks at every turn! A few of the comments I'll cite come from a wide swath of generations. One 25 year old sales person complained to his general sales manager: "We're supposed to be sales people and yet we spend 95% of our time NOT SELLING!!" His manager agreed with him and they've both since moved on to other positions and "greener pastures" so to speak. Another 67-year old gentleman who had actually owned bought and sold several radio stations in his time and was one of the true "masters" of new account development, once yelled to me:

"Can you imagine being intimidated.......by a COMPUTER?!!!!" Indeed I can Jim and indeed I have been, innumerable times! The 'catch phase' at one of my most recent positions was always a statement that began with: "IT WON'T LET ME…." And went on to describe a computer issue, usually related to a huge network of computers, all routed through some central office where an attempt at e-mailing a co-worker in the cubicle next to you took 10 minutes as the message was re-routed and re-routed again through Iceland, Singapore, the Bahaman islands, Atlanta…well, you get the idea. At some point you have to ask yourself the question as to whether these machines are supposed to be tools we use to facilitate our job or instead are our "masters?" "In charge of us" instead of the other way around?!!!

A BIG ROUND OF APPLAUSE FOR MR. JERRY DEL COLLIANO

One of my mentors for this book and one of the 'masters" of this business, a category I've always tried to learn as much from in every stage of my career, is Mr. Jerry Del Colliano. Jerry's long and distinguished radio career spans several decades and includes a major battle relating to his ownership of a recognizable publication called: "INSIDE RADIO." He traded multimillion dollar suits with the biggest of the consolidators, came out on top and now publishes a daily blog called INSIDE MUSIC MEDIA. I encourage anyone interested in the business to "Google' it, and subscribe to his daily posts for some incredible insights and foresights into the business past, present and future.

I'm extremely fortunate that Jerry has given me permission to quote from several of his past posts, or to at least paraphrase some of his material. Much of what he posts daily for free is actually quotes and information from his huge legions of followers and observers in the business or those who have left the business with graphic and vivid personal experiences. There may be some 'quotes within quotations' listed here. Jerry' personal credentials include:

> Advisor to New media & Broadcasting
> Consultant to Higher Education
> Clinical Professor Music Industry
> University of Southern California (04-08)
> BLOG:
> http://www.insidemusicmedia.com

You'll hear his own words, research, and observations. But you'll also hear stories and reports taken right from publications such as the Wall Street Journal. You'll also hear from a wide variety of other sources including those from radio and industry people all over the United States. This whole project has been basically MY story and now we're going to open up to a much more expansive world view.

A few things you'll experience that will illustrate that my personal approach to radio advertising has been pretty much on the mark, if I may pat myself on the back one last time(it's starting to hurt, but I feel it's important for the overall perspective!) are not limited to but include:

1. The loss of the live, local content, and live, local on air personalities, that both listeners as well as advertisers crave, and have always craved since the beginning of broadcasting. I cite my immediate embracement of the "live read" during my first years with Great Dane Media in Schenectady, New York, which basically kicked off the live endorsement phenomena there in my partnership

with Mike O'Leary, Myrna, and "Uncle Don" at "WFZ" news/talk.

2. The increasing value of not only The Internet itself, but all of the technological innovations it has spawned with the "I-Pods" personal data devices, delivery systems, and how they've led directly to the "on-demand" and "shortened attention spans" and immediate control over all informational content. And I'm not just talking about the "Generation Y" group of 80+ million people, but the "Generation X, "Baby Boom" and even the 65+ crowd all joining them in embracing these recent wonders of our age! You'll recall how in early 1995 I actually introduced 'THE INTERNET' to great Dane media and Larry Gronski, who as you also might recall, shook his head back and forth in a dismissing fashion and admitted, once I pressed him for an explanation, that he 'didn't see any future" in this recent innovation. Actually we're lucky that Al Gore invented the Internet, at least according to Al himself! Did you realize that it was actually "invented" by folks inside the United States Pentagon in the early 1960's? That's when the linking of vast computer systems began to take place for the nation's alert status in case of a military attack. I will say right here and now that this last statement itself ifs probably incorrect; it's just my own, relatively ignorant 'shot" at it. Someone reading this will most likely prove me wrong and cite an even earlier 'inventor.' Just please don't tell Al Gore that. I'd hate to break is heart!

3. The shortening of the attention span of the entirety of civilization. This was the rationale behind my employment of educational medical 'vignettes' or mini-infomercials, thanks to the teachings of one "master"

named Peter Vincelette. Aside from the "Welcome to another segment of WORD OF MOUTH" or the ending in which a different voice told you to: "….and be sure to listen for the next segment of WORD OF MOUTH!" the whole of the 'content' of these educational vignettes was just 45-seconds, and intended to raise the quality of the normal 'selling in your face" run of the mill 'sales pitch' to a purely education tidbit format, to give the listener some free medical, or legal, or real estate advice—that everyone loves, for "free" of course and to "POSITION" the advertiser as a leading expert in their field without the aggravation of the 'sales pitch' or "hurry on down here" pressure that no one really likes since they feel is if they're somehow being manipulated. There are many books out there about advertising as "positioning' such as those by Reis and Trout—two of my favorite authors.

In any case, please strap yourself in for the intellectual ride and eye-opening experience of your life as we selectively explore some of the information I was so very fortunate to learn from INSIDE MUSIC MEDIA. It's no longer, just MY story. It's YOUR story as well if you are either in the business as an employee, an advertiser, or a listener---the three main groups that the 'consolidators' all claimed to be their main customer groups---the three main groups who saw their dreams, their incomes, their careers, their advertising goals, and their very lives completely destroyed, hundreds and hundreds of thousands of times over!!

CHAPTER TEN

A QUICK REVIEW

Within the content of a few recent blogs from INSIDE MUSIC MEDIA we've seen the stark reality of pre-packaged bankruptcies as several of the biggest consolidators can no longer meet their staggering debt loads, the economic collapse only serving to accelerate the inevitable.

And we've seen the "Disney model" of success in continuously reaching successive generations as the younger kids fall in love with Snow White, Mickey Mouse, Bambi, Wall-E, the theme parks, and then in their pre-teen years watch Hanna Montana on the Disney Channel and then naturally move on in their later teen years to High school Musical in theaters. The process then repeats over and over as the "kids become older "kids" and have kids of their own. CEO Bob Iger's brilliance in bringing Apple's CEO Steve Jobs into the tent ensures a continuity of innovation well into the future and beyond anything that TV, radio, or the newspaper industries have come close to matching.

You've seen the comparison to the Toyota Prius as a comparison to radio be stuck in a 'gas powered' world while creativity and new technologies past them by. It's obvious that a much greater percentage of radio's operating budgets will have to be allocated to new media in 2010 and even more in 2011 and beyond. One radio staff can sell both terrestrial radio as well as the digital content. It's the same advertisers, make it the same staff embracing and presenting both.

Again to quote Jerry, "Hire back the talented people who were let go while radio was 'bonehead sizing'—that is kicking out the people who could help them the most. If a surgeon could help you return to health, would you walk into her office, abuse her, insult her, take away her x-ray machines and nurses and then say "return me to good health"? But that's what the CEO's have done to the very people who could have saved them."

"There is still an available audience for radio, but radio CEO's are tempting fate again by making wholesale cutbacks in talent, local programming, and a live presence in each market. How long can these listeners remain loyal when they're vulnerable to new media initiatives that have captured younger demographics?"

"Radio listeners want local programming, WITH personalities. Radio consolidators are moving in the opposite direction—a fatal mistake. Give the talent a percentage of the show's revenue. Come up with shorter shows. Make nights and overnights as special as mornings. All night shows could be magical again. Do something about the abysmal commercial load problem—fix it.

Many of you know I favor the content-commercial-content-commercial approach—not stacking the ads in two or three stop sets. All of us—not just the next generation—have shorter attention spans. Stop and start is your new best friend." I know that this is all a part of the entire world's knowledge base doubling every six months whereas it used to take 20 years. Reinventing the "live read" is the future. I've seen it perform magic form Schenectady New York to Tampa Florida. A morning team that was kicked off their show is now doing pod casting. Dave & Geri in Grand Rapids are making the live read a real money maker with their endorsements and providing their pod casts on demand. They're making their shows full of local community involvement, local news, and monetizing their show with live endorsements. If you take a hint from podcasting you'll see why broadcasting has to become more personal. The days of "All Ryan Seacrest All the Time" are over before they even started. Inside Music Media from July 15th states that 'available radio listeners want intelligent entertainers---who know about the content (music, news or talk—depending on the format. You can't do herky jerky radio jive in this era of great change and connect with today's listeners."

Now this is truly frightening for anyone "in" radio. A recent study quoted in INSIDE RADIO said "there will be no radio growth until 2015! You can't last that long! And there's no guarantee there will all of a sudden be growth again even six years from now!"

Social media is everything today, bigger than The Internet upon which it was built it now looms larger than any form of traditional media in scope or impact. It receives such intense concentration that many states have banned texting while driving, the weekly magazine THE WEEK's cover calling it "death by texting." Remember the train conductor who "texted" a dozen lives out of existence as he "texted" his way right into another train? Studies have shown that a motorist is something like 23 times more likely to crash while texting than in a normal driving situation. I personally know two female employees in the same company within the same 90-day period who were "T-boned" as some bonehead blew through a red light and smashed into them while in the middle of a text. That's two gals within the same 80-employee company in the SAME situation within the same 90-days! "The future is not computers, not the Internet by itself, not even the wonder of a cell phone. No, the future is social networking.

Not just by the pod cast to these mobile devices, or having them available on demand to accommodate all of our harried lives and shorter attention spans brought about by the exponential increase in new technologies, as a August 27th blog of INSIDE MUSIC MEDIA states, "Radio Needs video." Video streaming has been growing in popularity especially in the last year or so. "There's a new research study out from Ipsos mediaCT's MOTION that is picking up on a trend that radio people should consider and understand. Americans with access to the Internet are now streaming more TV shows and movies than at any previous time in history---26% streaming a full-length TV show and 14% a movie within the last 30 days alone(an increase of DOUBLE that of September 2008)."

Hulu, the replacement for TV for the next generation is a growing and popular means of watching ad-supported video programming. Advertisers won't take long to figure this out. "A blatant ad on YouTube actually gets better results. This commercial has over 700,000 views" and you can see why it definitely leaves the viewers craving more.

In Jerry's view "the new radio is podcasting because it cooperates with the inevitable—that is, short attention spans. The new talk radio is podcasting. But if talkers think they're going to do their radio shows for an iPod and not make substantive content and formatted changes, they will not transfer to the new media successfully. "Talk Radio" will be talk podcasting---45 minutes or less, and they will need compelling content, because here's the challenge with podcasting—forming a daily habit. Jerry's clients Dave and Geri report that downloads from their new age "morning" podcast" peak in the morning but nighttime downloads almost equal morning downloads. The morning show is now in essence—on demand—and their fans download the content at these two times in great numbers. "It's quite obvious that a whole generation has become used to being, and demands to be, in control of their content."

I recently bough a high-tech printer/fax/ copier, scanner and the teenage check out girl asked if my friend who was with me as a technical advisor and I were going into business for ourselves. I said: "No we're actually a new musical group working on our first album." She was impressed and said "Wow, really?!" My friend laughed and said 'she actually believed you!" As the smile disappeared from her face I said: "No, really" and then handed her a business card with my personal marketing website: www.bob-curran-consultant.com. It currently contains about 6 of my original tunes. I told her to go ahead and download some music if she wanted to. She answered:

"I hope it's free, I don't want to pay for downloading anything!" I assured her it was and we checked out. But that one little exchanged proved a much greater principle.

Again, according to INSIDE MUSIC MEDIA: "When they want to READ something they expect to click and see text. When they want to HEAR something, they expect to touch and get audio. When they want to SEE something, we have trained them to click and get video. If 'radio' (whatever that becomes in the future) can't do all THREE of these things, it has no future in the digital world." Amen, Jerry and INSIDE MUSIC MEDIA!!

CHAPTER ELEVEN

WE DON'T WANT TO 'GET UGLY' BUT WE'RE DESCRIBING UGLY SITUATIONS SO LET'S GET IT OVER WITH AS QUICKLY AS POSSIBLE AND BACK OUT INTO THE SUNSHINE ASAP!

From a post on INSIDE MUSICE MEDIA from July 11th, 2009.

"What do you get when you fire most of your local employees, revert to using voice tracking or cheap outside programming, manage from corporate headquarters, spy on stations and treat engineers like they are not necessary? No local radio—or as I like to call it—Nocal radio. You could call it knuckleradio because you'd have to be a knucklehead to do what radio CEO's are doing in the name of economies of scale. The three largest groups—Clear Channel, Cumulus and Citadel—are leading the way (if you could actually use the term 'leading' to describe this self-immolation). Believe me, the other small groups are falling all over themselves to adopt the same destructive and shortsighted policies as you will see."

I'll paraphrase a few examples and I've witnessed them all personally.

1. Playing offensive videos at "sales meetings." I saw this myself when a national rep firm visited our stations Schenectady, New York in 1995. They played Alec Baldwin's rant from 'Glengarry Glen Ross', the 1992 movie about the behind the scene workings of a real estate business. I saw it personally. The clip is loaded with insults and obscene language—some directed at the alternative life style of other employees with children. This was what they actually thought to be 'motivation?' Our Vice president and general manager, Michael, did jump all over it, damning it in a follow up meeting the next day but the damage had been wreaked upon us and the horse was out of the barn—nice try with the door, however, Michael! MORE SELLING TIME needlessly and negatively flushed down the nearest toilet!

2. Raising rates by 20% to cover losses. I've seen the pattern many times. You pound on the sales force and being the top flight professionals they are, they 'walk.' The top 10-15% of sales people rarely have a resume' handy or remotely up to date. They don't need to since they're ALWAYS in demand. "Sales folks on the streets are already

cringing as their prospects are hurting so much many are already skipping radio advertising at existing rates. Talk about being disconnected from your advertisers. Now is the time to cut rates—not during economic booms." Force your best people to leave, this produces less revenue. Then pound harder on a smaller staff for more sales, you lose more good people, and the pattern continues. What's that definition of "insanity' we've revisited quite a few times so far?

3. "Clear Channel's Goal: no one in the building on weekends." I haven't personally experienced this myself and it's a good thing since I'm a 7-day week man. I go into the office EVERY WEEKEND 52 weeks out of the year. When the majority of your time is NOT SELLING but being a 'clerk" you need the extra time to actually do a funny thing called "SALES' and/or "SALES PREPARATION!" What an odd idea, huh?

4. Father's Day Weather—one day late.

Let's quote directly from both INSIDE MUSIC MEDIA but one of those 'quotes within a quote' directly from a totally disgusted executive. "Clear Channel's high-rated WSRZ-FM, Sarasota, Florida, 60's70's hits, was plugging along, no back announcing, no local content, totally on automatic, when every hour, the recorded weather talked about the expected high tomorrow—FATHER'S DAY!! Seems someone forgot to update the weather since Father's day was two days in the past. Another fine example of serving the community's needs.

No harm done. No one got killed by a tornado this time---just voice tracking egg on your face."

Other examples include the whole industry completely dropping the ball on the day that Michael Jackson died. One or two hardy souls made it into the empty, pre-programmed studios and were able to piece together a few quick tribute songs but the industry as a whole dropped the ball like a drunken NBA mascot. One veteran broadcaster spoke about a female DJ bragging that she was actually in the studio taking the phone calls, as if it was supposed to be a 'bonus' for the audience. The "trick" I've heard about from some DJ's in the Tampa Bay area is to set the phones on 'automatic busy signals' as if the "lines are jammed' when actually there's only an empty studio and a pre-set busy signal for the caller to hear over and over. There are reports gushing in from all over the country about the lack of station identification. Just a ton of 'that was….this is.' That's just clowns having jocks do generic voice tracks that run on multiple stations. "Plus there's no weather, no local happenings, no local comments about artists appearing…nothing. That's your new local radio for you."

Jerry compared a historical event when he was recently in New York on September 17th regarding the massacre at Long Beach in 1782 as he stood beside the sign commemorating a massacre by Tory raiders. "Makes me think of the massacre at Clear Channel and Citadel that has ruined the lives of thousands of good and talented people while depriving loyal listeners of the excellent local product we know we can offer them" he mused on that day's blog page. Another disgusted, totally demoralized sale person wrote: "Try not making your goals at 8%....try working in an environment where you are selling across the cluster and competing for what was once sacred round that AE's developed on their own and are now open for who ever can sell it gets the cut or in this case the split. You have to share the business with another station in your building. Granted if it is new business you can own it but you have to watch your fries because that makes you a target. It is hunting season in the building and everything is fair game." What did I call this sickening phenomenon in a previous chapter? The "Gimme gimme, take-take, me-me mine-mine!!" inner workings? I've heard it said so many times; the godamn ENEMY is supposed to be "out there!!"(The competing radio stations) NOT sitting a few cubicles away in your own company!! "Worker against worker. Stress that is impacting the health of the sales force. Desperate consolidators." I can't tell you how many sleepless nights I've endured at the hands of some of these animals! I keep hearing the phrase everywhere lately and it's really starting to sink in: "Life's too short!"

Here's a quote from a Cumulus sales rep who escaped. I guess that they "recently instituted a new business requirement wherein AE's are expected to put 3 new accounts or $9,000 in new business per month on the air. Any AE's that don't fulfill this requirement will lose one of their billing accounts. AE's that don't generate any new business in 4-month period are subject to termination. It's sickening...." Now where have I heard that before? OH yes. That was basically the language of "the threat" that caused me to leave a successful career and drive 1,300 miles to Florida in 1999. I KNEW it had a very familiar ring! As Jerry encapsulated it:

"Things are so wacky in radio right now—no one is watching the future."

"Please re-read the last line. Please."

"No one is watching the future."

"What about the app-driven free/premium Spotify music service when it comes to the U.S. by year's end— threat or not? Or the dilution of personality radio in favor of voice tracking? Or the effect of podcasting as it grows with ex-radio personalities. Or the new Apple tablet that is rumored to be in the pipeline as the next entertainment device to rival the iPod or iPhone? What effect on radio?" Here are a few of his POSITIVE plans of actions:

1." Set sales goals but don't micromanage. Autonomy and the feeling that employees are given the tools to do their jobs are more important.

2. Let stations control the pricing based on ratings, the competitive situation and marketable personalities— not corporate.

3. No need to increase commissions, but restore the previous levels so they can make a living. And recall that misguided policy of docking salespeople for not bringing in the amount of new business you think they should. The reason that companies like Cumulus are about to meltdown in the next two quarterly revenue periods is a direct result of policies like this.

4. Read Dale Carnegie's "How to win Friends and influence People"". What he means is to get the very basics of what we call today 'people skills!!"

THERE WERE WAYS AND THERE ARE WAYS OF HOW CONSOLIDATION COULD HAVE WORKED

From the September 22nd INSIDE MUSIC MEDIA daily post:

"I never for even one minute thought that radio consolidation would work from the get go."

"But even I didn't believe that radio consolidation would have turned out this bad."

"It didn't have to be this way. All the power didn't have to wind up in the hands of a few radio execs worshiping at the feet of Wall Street bankers. There could have been a 'Plan B' just in case something went wrong—like a recession or an election where elected officials would put the brakes on further consolidation. The consolidators didn't have to borrow so much to buy stations they coveted at artificially inflated prices and astronomical interest rates."

Or, in my own experience, I'd like to add paying too much for the broadcasting rights to a sports team at the bottom of the pile and then threatening and beating the hell out of the brightest and best sales professionals and eventually driving them out the door since you made their lives miserable. Are you listening, Mr. Hitler-wanna be?!

"Consolidation could have worked if regulators and legislators hadn't given away the entire radio industry to a few greedy people. In effect radio consolidation was the forerunner to the greed that destroyed the greater economy."

Now THAT'S a statement that deserves some pondering as well as some historical perspective!!!

Don't forget that it all began with the Federal Telecommunications Act of 1996, right after I entered the business in Schenectady, role playing my heart out on Christmas Eve in 1994!!

"Imagine if….

1. The cap on stations that could be owned by one company in any given market was two stations. You pick them, two AM's, two FM's, one of both. This would have preserved the local feel of radio by guaranteeing that one owner from Texas wouldn't monopolize radio in every major market."

2. If each radio station by law had to have its own general manager, sales manager, program director, chief engineer, etc. No joint staffs that have proven to be no more effective other than to save the owners money. But that was a vicious cycle anyway (Now remember my own words from earlier in this chapter!)---save money at the expense of people, put out a lesser product, cut more people. Wait until you see the next round of cuts that clear channel, Cumulus, Citadel and their followers will start making before and through the end of the year. Obviously, a lean mean operation is becoming more mean than lean."

3. The two stations you could own in a market had to run separately and compete with each other. No synergies of scale, no national repeater radio". If you think that can't be done just think of the destruction of repeater radio that has no appeal to

the next generation and even erosion of listening by older audiences.

4. What if at least 80% of the programming had to be locally produced?" How much more fresh, local, and exciting would be the product?

5. "If public affairs and/or news programming were once again required to hold a license of the public trust?" And license renewals were mandated every three years with owners having to substantiate this?

6. There would be no need for any "Fairness Doctrine" with some many divergent opinions.

There's much more, but the 'bottom line(pun intended) would mean that owners under this kind of 'consolidation' would have stayed out of debt because responsible consolidation means having the skills to operate the local stations NOT just the ability to talk bankers into financing the acquisition of more radio properties. And it would mean an industry that wasn't dying before its time. Instead the model that didn't work was the one that these greedy bastards have adopted and been saddled with for over 13 years with no hope in sight.

"What a pity.....Management guru peter Drucker always said consolidation doesn't work. What makes radio CEO's smarter than Peter Drucker?" Thanks again Jerry, for some brilliant insights that all really hit close to home for me personally and that I've lived through for those 13 years!

CHAPTER TWELVE

CA'MON, LET'S GET HAPPY!

As I've said from the beginning, I don't want all of this to be a slamming of a great industry with a long and glorious history of success, and a great track record for entertaining a multitude of generations. So let's once again consult with INSIDE MUSIC MEDIA for some moves to make from "the professor" himself on how to save radio now.

These are urgent moves since "there is little time to waste righting the ship from the ravages of radio consolidation." Think about these very positive and productive ideas and then let's relate them to what the advertisers of the world now seek. After all, they, through their sales people and entire stations' team efforts are paying all of the bills. (I don't care what that loud-mouth, selfish-psycho, "radio-voice" yelling phony, "Tom" feels like yelling from his office. He's never brought in a penny of revenue, only proficient at helping spin the "one-a-month" revolving door at WFZ.)

1. "Negotiate with the record labels to gain advantageous rates for any terrestrial radio station doing new media projects." Radio has always enjoyed a performance tax exemption since it was the platform upon which new and existing artists received all of their exposure in the first place and pumped up sales in music stores. Artists were then able to further rake it in at concerts, merchandizing their own products, etc. But the music lobby, very powerful in nature is going after radio stations by lobbying Congress to back the performance demand for repeal of radio's exemption. One major consolidator has a half a BILLION interest payment coming due and is selling stock in a frenzy to keep afloat. More expenses in this recession will be a killer. If this is inevitable then try to get something back in return. Something like low, long-term rates for broadcasters who want to start new content streams on the Internet. Since this where the industry is going NOW is the time to lock in such rates.

2. Small Operators and small ownership. This has already been discussed as well as the benefits of such a move to the operators, listeners and advertisers. What a time for the National Association of Broadcasters (NAB) to address as well as embrace the needs of the small and medium operators, who, according to INSIDE

MUSIC MEDIA, "are going to have to mop up the mess Clear Channel, Citadel, Cumulus, and some predecessors have left for them.

It's all going to come down to smaller operators doing local radio well, like in the 'good old days.' "And doing original content as webcasters, mobile content providers and social network engineers." Yes, give a break to smaller operators moving in to save radio. "Loans for Locals" rather than "Cash for Clunkers."

3. "Consolidation as it was implemented was wrong and didn't work." Some regulation is needed but not in its current, self-destructive form. As previously mentioned as to how it relates to deregulation, there will be no need for any ridiculous "Fairness Doctrine" because there will be enough divergent opinions to serve the reasons behind such a doctrine and hey, we STILL get to keep our freedom of speech! Enough people fought and died for it. How about THAT as a bonus?

4. Get favorable podcasting royalties if podcasting is to be a major part of the "next radio." Have you seen a lot of 'boom boxes" lately or is everyone you see tethered to an iPod or other mobile device or laptop? Now is the time to both launch and to 'kick start" the industry! And my absolute favorite from Jerry?

5. "Pitch a big tent to become the National Association of Broadcasters and Content

Providers." No longer just the "NAB" by an entity called something like the 'NABACP.' "There are 80 million new listeners coming of age in the next generation. It's fair to say they are not big radio listeners---they are mobile phone users, iPod owners and social networking devotees. Radio is morphing into other things and this is a good a time as any to welcome in new media to create one strong association for like-minded interests."

Do you want to see an example of an advertising agency that truly "get's it?" There is one right here in the Saint Petersburg area that I know of since they sent out tens of thousands of flyers which are now published public property and I don't believe they'll mind at all if I sing their praises a little bit. "Google" 'CEA MARKETING GROUP" right here in beautiful Clearwater, Florida. They're a full service advertising agency that recently created a brilliant campaign for our local GTE federal credit union, aimed at 12 to 22 years olds and heavily concentrating on "new" and 'social" media. They call it their "U22 campaign' and you can check it out at:

www.flavorofcea.com.   Their slogan is "A new Flavor of Advertising" and it is richly deserved and to be commended!

"WHAT RADIO ADVERTISERS NOW WANT?"

This important tome is truly hot off the presses as of November 4th, 2009's post. By now we've seen that the radio industry is truly being hammered by the recession but it's also being beaten into the ground by its "inability to hold rates." I can remember stations easily getting $250 per minute rates (I worked at one for 5 years) during 2004-2008 but now groups, sweating all the way up the chain of command to "make their numbers' are "prostituting the industry's overall clout." Cheap packages, all day "phone-a-thons" in which inventory is just about given away, and other 'drop your drawers' tricks recently didn't even themselves work in late 2008 when I heard dozens of reps saying I had at least SIX "sure things" that surely blew right up in their faces and declined to buy, even at giveaway rates! One girl, who got only one out of her six 'sure things'—typical of the expectations and then disillusionment of that "boiler room" day said: "It just proves that nobody has any money!" (by the way, amid the speakers pounding out rap music and the dollar signs and other baubles hanging from all over the ceilings, it was determined that some poor soul who had been with the company for 13-years would be 'bounced down three flights of stairs and out into the parking lot on his ass!) ; Metaphor again employed freely.

"That's why now you're beginning to see radio as more of an add-on to other media buys. Being part of a total ad package including, say, television, print and/or new media isn't new. What is disturbing is the cheap price radio is getting to round out advertisers media packages." Those $250 rates are now going out the door at $80 to $100 each. It's not funny anymore. "Unfortunately there is not much that can be done about cutting radio rates. Stations have too much inventory, are too willing to sell on the cheap. Their best inventory has been fired—air personalities.

"ADVERTISING AGE' is a publication that often hits it right in the bull's eye regarding industry trends. This recent article says that what advertiser's want are LIVE READS! A truism I stumbled upon in 1995 in Schenectady, New York when I teamed up with Mike O'Leary! Mike by the way was hired away at 10 times his pay by WABC in New York City and is now even further up the food chain, in national syndication. I might be a tad brazen, but it was all of those 11 different new advertiser's and Mike's live reads that I sold incessantly that was at least a teeny, tiny part of what got him noticed from the 'big boys' in New York City. If you have ever heard a good live read it employs what everyone in the business, on either side of the desk, will tell you are the most effective form of advertising---word of mouth! In a live read the announcer fully believe in the product, has visited the business in person, knows the owner, the manager, the staff personally, and generally uses the product or service themselves. This "genuine belief" (usually unscripted or working merely from 'bullet points') comes across like your best friend sitting across from you in a restaurant and raving on and on about a great experience they've recently had with a particular product or service.

Compared to a 'canned' announcer's voice, pacing the wording perfectly exactly fit the 60-seconds a live read is the top of the flagpole sitting on the tip of the mountaintop in advertising. I know it. I've seen it, and I've earned hundreds and hundreds of thousands of dollars personally from it. In addition to creating some very happy and extremely log-term and loyal advertisers! Jerry?

"CBS and Clear Channel are more than willing to accommodate them. That's right, two radio groups that have fired or voice tracked their local talent into oblivion are now, if we are to believe what we read, pitching live reads to interested radio advertisers.

As the article points out, in the early days of radio the personalities or DJ's were paid to talk about toothpaste, cigarettes or local sponsor's businesses and services. They had credibility because---and this is important—they had the two big "L's."

Liked and Local." And yes, you guessed it—Clear Channel is packaging their favorite local/national personality, Ryan Seacrest as one of their premier live readers. Somehow you you get the feeling these consolidators don't understand live reads."

You have to wonder just how connected the 'endorsers' are to their products. They still get their endorsement fees, but credibility? That's another matter. One consolidator said that it will use local DJ's to do live reads on its streaming stations. Nope. Streaming stations are not personality driven so that goes right out the window. One corporate media client buyer, who employs live reads, said that "with a radio station, its most valuable asset is its DJ talent so marrying our client's brand with Clear Channel in a lot of key markets made a lot of sense." "What?!! A radio station's most valuable asset is its DJ talent? Have these advertisers turned on a radio lately? The radio industry is firing morning show talent at a blinding speed. Where they are not fired, morning show budgets are cut and sometimes their on air partners are eliminated. Morning shows (and other day parts) are being imported from other markets to save money.

There's that "saving money" thing that's been haunting us throughout this book! These consolidators better hope that their buyers continue to NOT listen to radio or else they will be snagged. They are probably on their laptops, Blackberries, or iPods." Have advertisers heard about voice tracking? And some stupid advertisers are falling for it." Jerry continues in this vital November post:

"I blame radio advertisers as much as I do hapless CEOs for the game we're now playing. It made sense in the past. Build local popularity and the personalities' popularity transfers to local clients." (And maybe into national syndication like my very talented buddy, Mike O'Leary, originally in Schenectady, pounding away for something like 75k per year previous to his live reads).

Then radio groups wanted to cut talent fees.

Then talent itself. What's wrong here is that radio fails to recognize that the thing it apparently hates is what advertisers apparently want—popular DJ'S" (or talk show hosts.)

Keep all radios away from advertisers or they'll find out.

Wait,

They'll find out anyway—when their local live reads don't work. So if you're going to get into live reads, on air or online, remember these rules.

1. Live and Local—the best talent combination to deliver a message." The closest thing you can get to actual word of mouth!

2. "Try not to record them—listeners know. Even Paul Harvey's listeners knew when he pre-recorded a "live" read.

3. Mary the talent to the client." I personally performed 11 different 'marriage ceremonies' between Mike in Schenectady and his clients. "Dearly beloved, we are gathered here today......." Well, you get the idea.
4. Adequately compensate the talent.
5. Believability is the goal and no one can be more believable than a personality in a local market.

But before you can do the sure fire steps to keep local money flowing into your station you've got to have the talent.

Oops!!"

CHAPTER THIRTEEN

ONE MORE QUICK DIP INTO "THE
UGLY POND" AND THEN SOME
GREAT NEW DEVELOPMENTS, "POST-
RADIO" AS WE CURRENTLY KNOW
IT, AND A SALUTE TO THE BEST
SALES PEOPLE IN THE WORLD...
RADIO PEOPLE!!

I first heard the term "ugly pond" from genius sales guru, Greg Bennett, when he described in one lecture about how to take a prospect into a situation where it's like you're both sitting there, watching a 'movie' in which the possible pro's and con's of the result of the prospect's decision are explored. The negative consequences were things like: "how about if it doesn't produce a significant return on investment?" Or "will my boss have me for lunch?!"---things like that to address each and every negative or objection up front, to eliminate them from the potential advertiser having second thoughts or riding a never ending merry-go-round of "maybe"—frozen in the decision-making process.

In this case 'the ugly pond' we'll briefly both quote as well as paraphrase comes from a very recent INSIDE MUSIC MEDIA post of November 1st, and it carries the opening title, a little unnerving, of "Radio's Hostile Workplace Uprising."

Now before you think for a moment that this is something like the opinion of just one person I have to state that I have in my possession a perfect example of these recent phenomena in the form of a letter to "corporate" from a completely disillusioned and demoralized employee. And this involves one of the biggest radio or media corporations in America today. Although the letter is by now, "viral" in nature; that is it's been sent around the world and forwarded within thousands upon thousands of e-mails, I hesitate to copy or publish it. I made sure to change every individual's name, radio stations, and the real name of the entire cluster, events, and the very timeline itself. However, it was so powerful in nature, and has now resulted in several lawsuits, employee and management terminations and other litigation, that I hesitate stepping into the "crossfire' even a great distance, until I've received a legal opinion on how to proceed. Let it suffice that it is the ideal and perfect illustration of what you are about to read. In every case I'll try to paraphrase or to encapsulate the situations in "the ugly pond" of this sad but inevitable workplace uprising. Now back to INSIDE MUSIC MEDIA, November 1st:

"It appears that we have the first signs of an uprising by abused radio employees protesting the increasingly pervasive hostile working environments they are being forced to tolerate. The post talks about "rumblings at Citadel, Cumulus, 'and, of course, Clear Channel where a lack of a solid example at the top has spawned little dictators terrorizing perfectly good clusters,"

I again ask you to use your imagination and picture that 20 MILLION DOLLAR proposal, on a CD that we salespeople couldn't open to find out what was on it. ("Can you imagine being intimidated…by a computer?!!—Jim Depalma, 67-year old former radio station owner again from 2004). And remember the 'dictator' with the picture of Hitler on his desk for inspiration, driving back to town after being embarrassed by corporate, tightly gripping the wheel while gritting his teeth in anticipation of "really coming down" on myself and my partner from another station who had put the proposal together, as we had been encouraged to do by the company, for not telling him about the 20 MILLION DOLLAR proposal on the CD we were unable to open. Remember 'dictator' Chick Duncan reacting my saying "you two guys made me look like a fool!!" Remember nonsense like that?! Well then please read on with INSIDE MUSIC MEDIA!

I continue from the previously- quoted words: "…….spawned little dictators terrorizing perfectly good clusters."

"Now, it's about to get uglier. Employees are speaking up and some are even retaining lawyers to stand up to unnecessary and unproductive working environments. Keep in mind that most people who have been the victims of workplace abuse, harassment or discrimination have had little option other than to complain and suck it up.

We're in a recession.

They need their jobs. What is sick is that the three worst radio groups---are about to get more trouble than they bargained for under the 'you reap what you sew' act."

"What I am about to outline here are complaints that have been made verbally and through written documentation to their employers about the growing hostile environment in radio. I'm proud of the fact that even faced with losing their jobs—or, in some cases, having already lost their jobs—most people have decided to give their allegedly abusive employers a chance to 'talk it out"(hugging it out is out of the question.) Some of those who have provided these accounts insist that 'this isn't an isolated incident.' Some are sadly eloquent."

"This isn't the first letter you've received from an ex-employee and all you do... (Or your human resources department will do is send copies of the letters back to the station) where they all stand around the station and everyone gets a good laugh. So let's all have a seat because this is going to be a laugh that should bring tears to your eyes.

They are not troublemakers, not malcontents. You can be the judge of whether you would like to work in an industry that treats its loyal and good employees like this:

1. Women discriminated against because they have children.
   Specifically, references made to female executives about the restraints of motherhood. In some cases female employees can only hold their noses and try to proceed with their career—even if they

are outperforming all the men in their clusters (Cumulus employee's allegation).

2. Retaliation when reporting workplace abuse. The communications between human resources and the complaining employee breached. One local GM reportedly laughing about having 'the girls" at their headquarters that tell him everything. Failing to follow through on complaints(Clear Channel employees allegation)

3. Illegal overtime being allowed for hourly workers. Labor Boards tend to be sympathetic to employees complaints because it is hard to believe that everyone's work can be finished between 8:30 and 5:30 in a business like radio.

4. Abusive language creating a hostile working environment. The "F" word is tossed around as if were 1965—a boys club. Many women—and men—find this language inappropriate in today's workplace and they may have a case when it is their turn to speak. Cussing out employees in front of studios (the employee cussed out was eventually fired (Clear Channel and Cumulus allegations.)

5. Now you're working/ now you're not severance packages. One clear Channel employee was allegedly told they had three months of severance to choose if they left which was allegedly withdrawn for no apparent reason when the employee was dismissed without severance.

6. Disgusting and unprofessional sales meeting tirades. In one instance I know about, there are allegations that the operations manager of a station

that flipped formats who solicited questions at a meeting, railed at several seasoned sales people who were concerned about their clients potential reactions to the timing. They were supposedly told that if they didn't like the f...ing rules then go play somewhere else. And market managers letting the entire staff have it when he started his meeting early and one account exec showed up at the scheduled time. (Clear Channel allegation)."

And it goes on and on from there but I've personally seen it all in some form somewhere and I'm simply too disgusted at this moment to keep typing and quoting the slime form this "ugly pond." But as INSIDE MUSIC MEDIA concludes, as well as so I in this 'ugly pond' chapter:

"There is always hope. The worst is over. Radio CEOs are being punished now as they must hand over control of their companies to the bankers who turned them into people without a conscience. There will never be a day when they are inducted into the Radio and TV Museum. History will give them what they deserve—shame for choosing personal wealth over the health of an industry that could have also given them an excellent living.

For those who have endured, the digital future will reveal itself in the coming years and the survivors will be an important part of it. It appears that consolidation may be giving away to mediation and litigation. And while the abusers are defending themselves in court, the employees may finally be able to move on."

"UGLY POND OVER" but quite appropriate as well as necessary as we now step into the sunlight with the final chapters, the next one called "FUTRE TRENDS COMING TO THE RADIO BUSINESS OR WITHOUT IT."

CHAPTER FOURTEEN

FUTURE TRENDS COMING TO THE RADIO BUSINESS, OR WITHOUT IT, AN EXCITING PIVITOL POINT IN HISTORY.

Read, listen, or watch any contemporary media outlet today and it goes without saying that we are indeed living in very historic times. We may be headed into a glorious, never-imagined future, full of happiness and prosperity. Or we may have once again failed to learn from history and be doomed to repeat it; "goose-stepping" our way into an oven while we yell "Sieg heil!" proudly throwing out a Nazi-like salute as we're rounded up like cattle, perhaps in small increments, but done nevertheless.

That's kind of a quasi-political statement or cultural observation. But what does it have to do with the future of "radio" as we know it today? In a post on INSIDE MUSIC MEDIA way back in May 18th, Jerry observed:

"I, like you, wish it could all be as good as it once was when radio was king and the record industry kept the hits coming. I knew it was over when I joined the University of Southern California faculty after selling INSIDE RADIO to Clear Channel. The students didn't like radio and didn't need the record labels. They still don't. And without retelling what you already know, it should suffice to say that the radio industry let the next generation get away on the watch of a handful of play-CEOs intoxicated with power."

The first chapter began with sad stories of some of the most talented radio people, being bounced out the door, listeners burnt and even injured by "money-saving" tricks like voice-tracking, people totally brutalized to the point of giving up on their jobs and even their lives. Some of the animals and their treatment of good, hard-working, very talented people were then showcased. But what do we do now moving forward?!!

"Here are a few ways that these talented people can take advantage of what consolidators have repeatedly rejected---the digital future."

1. PODCASTING. As mentioned several times, this is the 'new radio' or at least a necessary component of it moving forward. On air personalities, news staff, producers, writers, and even salespeople, who sometimes embody all of the above—are doing daily podcasts. This isn't just radio moved to podcasting. Again to quote INSIDE MUSIC MEDIA: "I'm speaking of a new relationship with your audience. Anyone can do a podcast for the hell of it. I'm talking

about a franchise that can be monetized through ancillary forms of sponsorship. The audience can grow through social networking."

You've seen the great example of Clearwater, Florida's CEA Marketing group and their "U22" campaign for the credit union!

"You own the franchise. As it grows you make the money. Only your audience can fire you. I've told you about a podcasting development client I have (former number one radio morning team) who went live in mid-June with the next iteration of radio. No music. Their mouths to your ear bud. Think Jean Sheppard." (You might want to "Google" that one.)

2. INTERNET STREAMING OF NON-TERRESTRIAL CONTENT. "There will be a market for unique programming not a jukebox. Today's jukebox is already loaded and running. It's an iPod. Internet streams will work when they have special programming done by qualified people who have earned the right to be on. There are plenty of problems here not the least of which is the expense of succeeding with music programming. A reader wrote to me the other day to say he had to take down a stream that gets 500,000 listeners a day because he couldn't pay the music licensing fees—another reason to fight the evil record labels. This is no time to throw cold water on what could be a hot new industry. In the meantime, stream what others have dared not to do. Use social networking to build and

maintain the audience. You own it. I can build an Internet station in a week—and make it better in a month. You can too."

3. HOW ABOUT INTERNET STATIONS FOR LOCAL RESTAURANTS, BUSINESSES AND OTHER RETAIL ESTABLISHMENTS? Jerry terms this: "a little twist on internet streaming that is an automatic money-maker. You own them and license them to the clients. It's professional and designed to be heard in the store by their listeners. Live 365 will do. Again, keep in mind the licensing fees and proceed with caution until that issue is finally resolved, but pitch companies on more than music in the store. Before opening, the programming is for the employees. When the doors open, it works in real-time for the customers. After hours, it's for the janitor or stock people. It's very affordable and I have a friend who does this and shows the client how to get their 'investment" money back by selling sponsorships to their suppliers.

There's a huge restaurant group in town, Tampa-based OSI restaurant Partners, which owns Outback, Carraba's Italian Grill, Bonefish grill, and other brands. There's a very accomplished, talented, former Avon executive, Liz Smith, who has just taken over as CEO of the chain. Do you think that with her background she'd be at least open to looking at a delivery system that played Australian music and commentary at Outback, Italian-themed music and content at Carraba's etc? Maybe I could combine the best of all worlds and have this music performed and pre-recorded by local artists playing this music, trying to be discovered and trying to break into the public consciousness and would do it for little or no compensation in exchange for all the exposure? Please don't anybody tell Liz. I want it to be a surprise! (L.O.L).

1. THE LOCAL NEWS SOURCE IDEA. "If you're a newsperson, writer, community affairs executive, or interested in ways to dispense information in a digital world, pick a town or city and become the "news source" for it—town meetings, crime, anything that goes on in that locale. Put it up on a website and, better yet, add an Apple app that people in that location can carry around on their phones to touch and connect with what's happening close to their homes in real-time. Monetize the app, the website and ancillary income streams that come from owning the franchise for Hoboken, New Jersey, or Newport Beach, California (or Saint Petersburg, Florida, for that matter!). Newspapers won't do it—they once did regional editions loaded with feature stories. Radio barely does any news. Own a town and get rich with your production, reporting, and social networking and Internet skills. Really adventurous? How about the new digital "newspaper" that everyone will read…"

2. IT WILL BE BLOGS!! I agree with Jerry that "it's not news websites—that's no business model. It will be blogs—special information on something that attracts a valued audience. But instead of

monetizing it by selling ads (something I think has peaked even when the recession ends, sell a subscription. That's right. I am nuts. I believe people will pay a reasonable fee for that which they crave—remember I said crave not like. In the past if you are an expert on gardening, you would have done a radio show, TV or newspaper column. Now you'll do a blog. And if it has passionate followers and you price it right, you'll make money and build revenue with your audience. Keep in mind I'm projecting this trend---its coming because it has to come. The Internet is a delivery system not the content."

3. FAMILY OWNED AND OPERATED! The mom and pop operations built this industry into a successful business before the consolidators made Gordon Gekko from the movie "Wall Street" look like Mother Teresa!" There's a friend of mine locally, whom I'm helping launch just such a locally-owned, locally programmed, very targeted medium to reach the 15-20% of the Tampa population who is Spanish-speaking or at least bilingual. "Funny about that isn't it? Local operators know radio. So if you want to buy a small station make sure its real small—and do local radio or TV. Not 24/7 music programming---anyone can get music about anywhere. The only operators that are even making it today are local mavens who have no or low debt and who do local radio. Look, radio will never be the growth business it once was but the one thing that could give it a breath of life—the consolidators

won't do or don't know how to do—local radio. I wouldn't invest a lot. Go LMA someone's station and show them what a pro can do. Seeing television is about to become radio—dead on arrival? Consider this…"

4. VIDEO—short video—is the feature. "Apple is going to come out with a new tablet pad sometimes referred to as an iPod that will continue to revolutionize the industry. There's a business here for talented producers. Informational shows, short-form dramas, entertainment series—it's what's next after YouTube and what's between here and Hulu. The website owned by a few entertainment companies to monetize online viewing of their TV shows. Except this idea is to create your own franchises—deliver it to whatever technology is available including computer screens, Apple TV, iPods and iPhones and whatever is next." How about one greatly overlooked idea that used to be radio during the 'British Invasion" during the "Beatle mania' ear of the early 1960's?

5. MUSIC DISCOVERY!! "Every iPod is a modern day jukebox or oldies station, so innovators are going to have to move beyond that. Radio doesn't—it just plays the same short playlists over and over. But there is room for knowledgeable people who can discover new acts, new artists, new songs and bring them into the pipeline" (even as the example I cited locally, it was over the speaker system at Outback steak house!) "You won't be making money on selling CD's

(although you may make some money from old world technologies.) Music discovery will be a business all to itself and it's fair to say the labels will sit this one out. The key is to go out and find the talent, sign them to royalty-free music agreements and then use whatever technology comes along to deliver it to the end user. It's in effect, the anti-record label."

There's oh so much more, and you can view it in real time by subscribing to INSIDE MUSIC MEDIA. The 'suits' and the double-chin bean counters, the dictators, and the jerks yelling in your face are surely on the road to their own destruction. They've bounced down and kicked a ton of talent to the street. They're now bumbling their way through these tough times! As Jerry put it: "once you get a taste for the potential, you'll be invigorated like never before."

I'll finish with a tribute to the people who have both made it all happen with hard, relentless work while enduring the abuse in spite of the maniacs that they work for. I'll end 'VOLUME ONE' with a tribute to radio people. 'VOLUME TWO' will be much more humor-oriented, with input from people who have been in the trenches for years and sharing their stories....the finest of the fine...RADIO PEOPLE!!

CHAPTER FIFTEEN

MANY SPECIAL WORDS OF THANKS
AND SINCERE APPRECIATION
AND A SALUTE TO THE BEST AND
MOST VALIANT PEOPLE IN THE
WORLD........RADIO PEOPLE.

When I voluntarily 'retired' from "Crux" Communications in Tampa in March of 2009, fully vested in their fully-funded employee pension program and holding a Certificate of Appreciation for "Five Years of Dedicated and Loyal Service", signed by the Chairman and CEO, I also left as the leader in digital sales, leaving over $48,000 on the books for 2009. And this was just by March 1st. I was also the oldest person in the 6-station sales force, and I believe, one of the oldest in the building, pushing 60. So I know that the new digital world coming to media can be embraced as well as utilized by sales people of any age, or at any level of their experience in the "entertainment business" which it all essentially is.

In fact, there's a "new sheriff" coming to town that has the potential to blow the old paradigms of 'broadcast" off the face of this earth! It's a product that Apple is developing right now. Again, according to the cutting edge knowledge from INSIDE MUSIC MEDIA,

"The next big competitor to radio, TV and the music industry is going to be what some term the Apple iPod. That may not be the name but here's what we're hearing. It's a handheld unit—larger than the iPhone or iPod and smaller than a laptop computer. It may download and play movies on the fly, be a cooler Kindle(digital book reader), display newspapers and magazines(probably in color), contain your pictures from iPhoto, allow you to use your apps and may have one or two other surprises from Apple CEO Steve Jobs such as display PDF's and store college textbooks.

You won't see an FM radio on it.

The New York Times recently gave some added credibility to the buzz that Apple is indeed planning to bring this product to market. I am hearing that the price will be around $800—could be slightly less—and rebates may make it a few hundred dollars cheaper as a phone contract will be required. That's a second phone contract in addition to what most consumers have now for texting, voice/and or surfing the Internet."

Am I shaking in my boots? Not the top digital sales leader in one of the biggest and most powerful radio clusters in Tampa Bay. As one of my inspirational coaches, noted psychologist, author, and lecturer, Dr. Wayne Dyer, has said many times, the Chinese symbol for 'crisis" is the exact same symbol for "opportunity." Thus within every potential crisis there lies an unlimited opportunity.

And who will carpe diem, or 'seize the day' as the translation form the Latin goes? Radio people!!

"The can-do spirit of radio people kicked into high gear even from the beginning when consolidators made promises to them that they couldn't keep. They said consolidation was a good thing. The "big boys" who reported to shareholders in their quarterly conference calls that they were going to build 'shareholder value.' Of course, as we discovered shareholders were the second biggest losers in radio consolidation, after the listener. Cost cutting took time and just as a cataract grows slowly to impair vision in one's eye, the snip-snip-snip of bean-counters weakened the fabric of local radio but many radio people couldn't see it. They just pushed on."

I'm proud to say that I was one of those people... radio people.

Even when I had to 'role play on both Christmas and New Year's Eve in 1994.'

Even after being threatened with losing accounts if I didn't sell this or that (.I was selling above average and actually leading in these categories!)

Even when a psycho with a picture of Adolph Hitler on his desk for 'inspiration' reacted to a 20 MILLION dollar proposal by spitting out hate and sick revenge upon his staff members.

Even when every single member of the staff in Schenectady, New York, thought they could 'talk down' and even 'act down' to the salespeople as being the lowest forms of scum existing on the earth (Even "little Mike" the studio gopher, and a 100% genuine loser!).

Even when monthly billing statements were intentionally and illegally manipulated by "accidentally" and regularly running out of postage each month) that the sales people would be robbed out of their hard-earned money!

Even when the brightest and best in the business were 'bounced down three flights of stairs and right out into the parking lot on their asses!

And it goes without saying that I have to agree with Larry Gronski, (my first sales manager) that radio sales people are the best trained in the world of sales. This is, of course, if you both accept and apply that training. And I did both with a passion. Remember motivational speaker, Don Bevridge, who pounded the podium and rattled the room by yelling: "And I'll tellya something else too! When management feels that it has to play policeman…you are ON (pound) YOUR WAY (pound) OUT OF BUSINESS!!" (Double-pound). The other point that Don made was that "got some great ideas do you? Well ANYBODY can come up with a great idea!! Where you people drop the ball is in the EXECUTION of your ideas!!!" As cluster general manager and regional V.P. Michael Warren, subsequently told me: "You are the master of the EXECUTION of your ideas!"

In my 15 years in this business, the first 10 of which I've recounted chronologically, bringing me up to the days just before I began my 5-year run of success at Crux communications, I've been extremely fortunate to have met and to have learned a lifetime of knowledge from some of the best people in any business….radio people!

I've quoted Jerry Del Colliano, "the professor" a great many times from his daily blog of INSIDE

MUSIC MEDIA that I encourage anyone and everyone to subscribe to for free for a continuing update as to how the radio business is rapidly morphing into something totally different than when I did the Christmas eve roll-play. And I can never thank him or praise him enough! Radio people!

I'd like to thank Mike "O'Leary" for a great mutual effort in kicking the live read program into the stratosphere at WFZ as well as every other 'endorser' on-air personality I've worked with in my career—always with total and complete success for the advertisers.

I'd like to thank on-air personality, Jeff Slater for the inspiration for the title of this book.

I'd like to thank all of the creative and studio people who did so much to "craft" our eventual "product", our radio commercials.

I'd like to thank all of the 'behind-the scenes" people in the Traffic, Continuity, secretarial, and sales support departments for their continued dedication to duty, often at wages that are well below what they truly deserve for their production.

I'd like to thank Don Bevridge for some great podium-pounding truisms.

I'd like to thank Mr. Chris Stonick for showing me a full day presentation on the art and the science of how to use radio as a fantastically effective tool in employee recruitment. I've made hundreds of thousands of dollars from it and penetrated into Bank of America, Pepsi Cola, and even General Dynamics and have gotten them all on the radio!

I'd like to thank Dr, Philip J. LeNoble for his program in which you are able to easily present and execute both annual sales contracts and even multi-annual contracts to quickly build your base and avoid having to reinvent the wheel each month to hit your numbers.

A very special 'shout out' to a man who has been my teacher, mentor, 'sun sei' and has uncanny and brilliant insights into the 'science of human behavior' as well as radio sales, Mr.. Matthew Rodriguez. That in itself was the equivalent to a 5-year media education of a college or even a post-graduate level!

I greatly appreciate the style and teachings of Mr. Pete Vincelette, who taught me how to elevate normal 60-second commercial to a whole new level by creating medical educational segments, or 60-second, mini-infomercials or vignettes.

And I truly appreciate people like Sophie Fry and Mike Anderson from "CSS"or the Center for Sales Strategy for years of ongoing instruction in analysis and sales approaches.

And of course, all of the great people I've worked with learned from ad benefited from, including management at every level during my career. The greatest and most resilient group of people in the world....radio people!

Dale Carnegie himself once made the statement: "Everyone in the world is my superior....in that I can learn something from them!" Thanks for reading "Volume One" of "DEAD AIR" and I sincerely hope you'll have a great and never-ending time laughing your way through "Volume Two!!"

RESPECTFULLY,
David Lear